DINOSAUR INFOSAURUS

Katie Woolley

WAYLAND
www.waylandbooks.co.uk

First published in Great Britain in 2021 by Wayland
Copyright © Hodder and Stoughton, 2021
All rights reserved
Editors: Elise Short and Grace Glendinning
Designer: Peter Clayman

ISBN: 978 1 5263 1729 2

Printed and bound in China

Wayland, an imprint of
Hachette Children's Group
Part of Hodder and Stoughton
Carmelite House
50 Victoria Embankment
London EC4Y 0DZ
An Hachette UK Company
www.hachette.co.uk
www.hachettechildrens.co.uk

The material in this book has previously been published in the following titles:
Dinosaur Infosaurus: Dinosaur Babies
Dinosaur Infosaurus: Dinosaur Bones and Fossils
Dinosaur Infosaurus: Gigantic Dinosaurs
Dinosaur Infosaurus: Killer Dinosaurs
Dinosaur Infosaurus: The Age of Dinosaurs

CONTENTS

THE AGE OF DINOSAURS

IN THE BEGINNING 8

WHAT A VIEW! 10

WHAT EXACTLY IS A DINOSAUR? 12

TRIASSIC DINOSAURS 14

JURASSIC GIANTS 16

CRETACEOUS KINGS 18

BIG AND SMALL 20

HOW DID THE DINOSAURS LIVE? 22

BETTER TOGETHER 24

ATTACK AND DEFENCE 26

THE END OF THE DINOSAURS 28

HOW DO WE KNOW ABOUT THE DINOSAURS? 30

DINOSAURS TODAY AND QUICK DINO FACTS 32

GIGANTIC PLANT-EATERS

GENTLE DINOSAURS 36

TINY AND TALL 38

GRAZING GIANTS 40

DINO DEFENCE 42

SAUROPOD HERDS 44

THE HEAVIEST SAUROPOD 46

SAILS AND SPINES 48

DOUBLE BEAM GIANT 50

BONES AND PLATES 52

THREE-HORNED GIANT 54

SUIT OF ARMOUR 56

CLAWED CREATURE 58

QUICK PLANT-EATER FACTS 60

KILLER DINOSAURS

DEADLY HUNTERS   64

BUILT TO KILL   66

DINOSAUR DINNERS   68

DINO GANGS   70

TERRIFYING T. REX   72

SCARY SPINOSAURUS   74

CUTE COELOPHYSIS   76

VICIOUS VELOCIRAPTOR   78

GRUESOME GIGANOTOSAURUS   80

GIANT YUTYRANNUS HUALI   82

FEARSOME FISH-EATERS   84

BURIED BONES   86

QUICK KILLER FACTS   88

DINOSAUR BABIES

EGGS OF ALL KINDS   92

JUVENILE DINOSAURS   94

TYRANNOSAURUS REX BABIES   96

STEGOSAURUS BABIES   98

TRICERATOPS BABIES   100

TROODON BABIES   102

PROTOCERATOPS BABIES   104

DIPLODOCUS BABIES   106

OVIRAPTOR BABIES   108

MAIASAURA BABIES   110

VELOCIRAPTOR BABIES   112

ICHTHYOSAUR BABIES   114

QUICK EGG-CELLENT FACTS   116

SEA AND SKY MONSTERS

PREHISTORIC NEIGHBOURS   120

MONSTERS OF THE SEA   122

INCREDIBLE ICHTHYOSAURUS   124

POWERFUL PLESIOSAURS AND PLIOSAURS   126

MIGHTY MOSASAURS   128

MEGA MEGALODON   130

THE BIG, THE BAD AND THE UGLY   132

EARLY MONSTERS OF THE SKIES   134

IMPRESSIVE PTERANODON   136

HUGE HATZEGOPTERYX   138

ENORMOUS WINGED QUETZALCOATLUS   140

PRETTY PTERODAUSTRO   142

QUICK FANCY FACTS   144

DINOSAUR BONES AND FOSSILS

THE WORLD OF THE DINOSAURS   148

BONE FOSSILS   150

TRACE FOSSILS   152

DINOSAURS AROUND THE WORLD   154

IGUANODON BONES   156

ANKYLOSAURUS BONES   158

STEGOSAURUS BONES   160

TRICERATOPS BONES   162

DIPLODOCUS BONES   164

VELOCIRAPTOR BONES   166

TYRANNOSAURUS REX BONES   168

SPINOSAURUS BONES   170

DINOSAUR DETECTIVES   172

GLOSSARY   174

INDEX   176

THE AGE OF
DINOSAURS

IN THE BEGINNING

Planet Earth has been around for a very long time – about **4.6 billion years**. Scientists divide this time up into chunks called eras. Dinosaurs lived during the **Mesozoic era**, which is split into three periods: Triassic, Jurassic and Cretaceous.

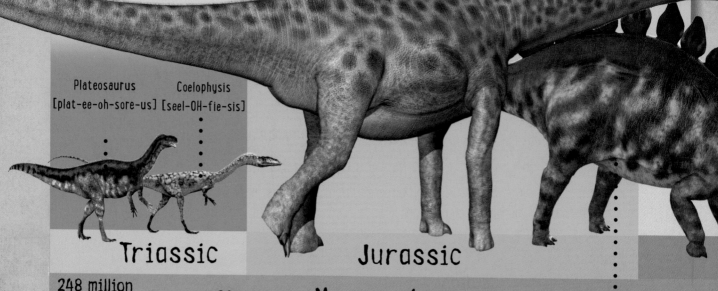

Plateosaurus
[plat-ee-oh-sore-us]

Coelophysis
[seel-OH-fie-sis]

Stegosaurus
[STEG-oh-SORE-us]

Triassic

Jurassic

248 million years ago (mya)

205 mya

Mesozoic era

142 mya

One of the **first dinosaurs** was **Nyasasaurus parringtoni** [Ny-as-a-SOR-us pah-ring-toe-nee]. It was the **size of a Labrador dog** and was discovered in Tanzania, Africa.

Dinosaurs shared their world with some **strange creatures**. **Eozostrodon** [ee-oh-ZOSS-troh-don] was a small, **egg-laying mammal** with short legs and a long snout – a bit like a **shrew**!

8

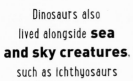

Dinosaurs also lived alongside **sea and sky creatures**, such as ichthyosaurs and pterosaurs.

Dinosaurs such as **Tyrannosaurus rex** and **Triceratops** thrived during the **Cretaceous period**. At this time, dinosaurs were **ruling the world!**

Diplodocus*
[DIP-low-DOCK-us]

• Tyrannosaurus rex
[tie-RAN-oh-sore-us rex]

Triceratops
[tri-SERRA-tops]

Cretaceous

Mesozoic era

65 mya

Earth is constantly changing. Today, the world is made up of seven continents but the earliest **Triassic dinosaurs** lived on one **supercontinent** called **Pangaea** [pan-JEE-uh].

• Triassic period
200 mya

• Jurassic period
145 mya

• Cretaceous period
66 mya

Human beings didn't exist until **62.5 million years** after the last dinosaurs walked the Earth!

9

*not to scale

WHAT A VIEW!

Dinosaurs had a very **different view of Earth** from the one we see today. They wouldn't have seen any human beings, buildings or roads and they wouldn't have heard or seen any aeroplanes in the sky.

Pangaea was surrounded by ocean. **Pangaea means all the Earth.**

Triassic dinosaurs would have looked out on the **hot, dry desert** of Pangaea. This may explain why they **lived close to coasts and rivers**, to be near **water**.

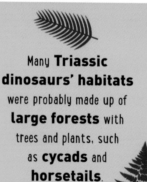

Many **Triassic dinosaurs' habitats** were probably made up of **large forests** with trees and plants, such as **cycads** and **horsetails**.

The first dinosaurs saw **very little colour** - probably just **greens** and **browns** as there were **no flowers** during the **Triassic period**.

Triassic trees were protected by very **tough needles**. Their spikey leaves put off hungry herbivores.

During the **Jurassic period**, Pangaea began to **split** into two. By the end of the Cretaceous period, Earth looked more like it does today. Its temperature had cooled.

By the **Cretaceous period**, Earth had burst into **colour**! Flowering plants arrived and more **mountains** appeared.

Some dinosaurs may have eaten **grass**. Fossilised grass has been found in **dinosaur poo**, known as coprolite.

Late Cretaceous dinosaurs, such as Iguanodon [ig-WHA-noh-don], would have seen **magnolias** and **buttercups**!

11

WHAT EXACTLY IS A DINOSAUR?

Dinosaurs were **reptiles** that walked the Earth for 165 million years. Scientists think there were as many as **1,500 different kinds!** About 700 have been discovered so far. The scientist Richard Owen was the first to use the word 'dinosaur' in 1842. It means terrible lizard.

At the beginning of the **Triassic period**, dinosaurs were just another **group of reptiles** in a world full of reptiles. By the end of the period, dinosaurs **dominated** the landscape for the next 140 million years.

About 65 per cent of all dinosaurs were herbivores. The rest were carnivores!

Dinosaurs were descended from archosaurs. The fiercest archosaur was Postosuchus [POST-oh-SOOK-us], a cousin of modern crocodiles!

Some dinosaurs walked on **two legs**. Others walked on **four**. They all walked with their legs **straight under their bodies** and not splayed out to the side like a crocodile's.

Fossil finds (see pages 26-27) tell us about specific dinosaurs. Dinosaurs are usually **named** after the **person** who found them, a particular **feature** or after the **place** in which they were discovered. **Medusaceratops Lokii** [med-u-sah-SERRA-tops lock-ee] had horns that looked like the snake hair of the Greek mythical monster Medusa.

We are learning more and more about dinosaurs all the time. When a **fossil** of **Iguanodon** was first discovered, scientists thought its spike was on its nose. We now know it was on its thumbs!

This dinosaur is a plant-eating **Aegyptosaurus**, pronounced ee-JIP-toe-SORE-us. Its name means Egyptian lizard.

Dinosaurs had **scaly skin**. Scientists say some had feathers as well.

This dinosaur is meat-eater **Spinosaurus**, pronounced SPINE-oh-SORE-us.

Most meat-eating dinosaurs belonged to a group called **theropods**. This name means **beast footed**.

Aegyptosaurus was a **sauropod** - a kind of **plant-eating dinosaur**. Like many other plant-eaters, it had a small head, long tail and long neck.

Meat-eaters had **sharp hooked claws** for finding food and protecting themselves.

TRIASSIC DINOSAURS

There were no dinosaurs at the start of the **Triassic period** but plenty of dinosaurs had arrived by the end of it. These dinosaurs lived in **hot, dry habitats**, such as the Petrified Forest in Arizona, USA. This area is full of the fossils of Triassic dinosaurs.

This is **Coelophysis.**

Coelophysis was a Late Triassic dinosaur. It lived about **220 mya**. It was **3 m long** – about the same size as a female **tiger**.

During the Triassic period, dinosaurs such as **Coelophysis** were **not at the top of the food chain**. Large reptiles called **archosaurs and phytosaurs ruled the land**.

Coelophysis walked on two feet allowing it to **run quickly and catch its prey**, such as **small insects** and **reptiles**.

Eoraptor [EE-oh-RAP-tor] lived about 228 million years ago. It was **smaller than Coelophysis.**

Eoraptor was only about a metre long. That's about the **size of a guitar**. But its sharp teeth and claws made it **a top predator**.

The fossil remains of a baby **Mussaurus** [moos-SORE-us] are some of the **smallest dinosaur skeletons** to have been found. This Triassic dinosaur **hatchling** could fit in the palm of an adult human's hand.

Among the first dinosaurs was **Saltopus** [SAL-toe-puss] – a very small meat-eating dinosaur found in Scotland. It was **no bigger than a cat!**

Early dinosaurs were not as big as later ones. But many dinosaurs had begun to evolve into bigger beasts by the end of the Triassic period. **Plateosaurus** reached about **7 m in length!** That's just a bit shorter than the length of a school bus.

JURASSIC GIANTS

As Pangaea began to break up during the Jurassic period, Earth's temperature cooled, **rainforests** grew and shallow **seas** formed. This period saw the arrival of large, four-legged plant-eaters – the **sauropods!** Many new dinosaurs emerged including Brachiosaurus, Allosaurus and Apatosaurus.

This is **Brachiosaurus**, pronounced BRAK-ee-oh-sore-us.

Brachiosaurus held its head very high to eat leaves on the tallest trees.

Brachiosaurus ate about **200 kg of leaves and twigs** every day. That's like eating **200 cabbages**!

 x200

Brachiosaurus weighed about **30-50,000 kg** - the same as **12 elephants.**

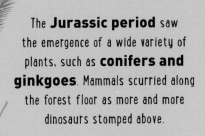

The **Jurassic period** saw the emergence of a wide variety of plants, such as **conifers and ginkgoes**. Mammals scurried along the forest floor as more and more dinosaurs stomped above.

As the number of **plant-eating dinosaurs grew**, so did the number of **large meat-eaters**. These mighty killers **dominated** the landscape, eating anything they could catch!

This large plant-eater is **Apatosaurus**, pronounced ah-PAT-oh-sore-us.

This fierce meat-eating dinosaur is **Allosaurus**, pronounced AL-oh-saw-russ. Its name means other lizard.

Its **long whip-like tail** acted as a **counter-balance** to its neck. It may also have been a good **defensive weapon**!

Apatosaurus was a Late Jurassic sauropod. It reached its full size at about 10 years of age and was **21 m long**. That's like seeing **10 male lions** standing in a line!

Allosaurus was a **fierce predator** during the Jurassic period. Its enormous size meant that it didn't shy away from **tackling big prey**, such as the large plant-eater **Stegosaurus**.

CRETACEOUS KINGS

By the end of the Cretaceous period, dinosaurs could be found on all seven continents. Dinosaurs had quickly adapted to their different habitats and their numbers had grown significantly. Dinosaurs were ruling the Earth!

Flowering plants began to grow during this time. The Earth came alive with colour! Dinosaurs started to share their world with **flying reptiles** - the pterosaurs.

This gigantic beast is **Argentinosaurus**, pronounced AR-gent-eeno-sore-us.

Two big Cretaceous beasts lived side by side. Argentinosaurus was a huge plant-eater. It was more than **three times bigger** than the **biggest meat-eater** at the time - Giganotosaurus!

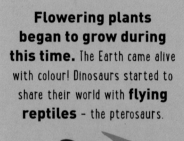

The **temperature** on Earth at the beginning of the Cretaceous period was much like the Jurassic period. Over the next few million years the temperature **cooled**.

Velociraptor [vel-OSS-ee-rap-tor] **was a vicious Cretaceous hunter.** Small, light and agile, Velociraptor was **built for speed**, which it needed to catch its prey. Its **bite was as powerful as a lion's!**

This hadrosaur is **Parasaurolophus**, pronounced pa-ra-saw-ROL-off-us. Its name means crested lizard.

This ankylosaur is **Euoplocephalus**, pronounced you-OH-plo-kef-ah-luss. Its name means well-armoured head.

Ankylosaurs were Cretaceous dinosaurs that were **built for defence**. They were covered in **spikes** and **horns**. Euoplocephalus even had special neck armour: several bony plates fused together in an arch-shaped block.

Hadrosaurs were the most common Cretaceous dinosaurs. They often had **strange head shapes** and odd-looking crests, possibly to **identify** members of their own species.

Large herds of dinosaurs like **Parasaurolophus** thrived during the Cretaceous period.

BIG AND SMALL

Plant-eaters, meat-eaters, big and small – there was a huge **variety of dinosaurs**. Some dinosaurs, like Diplodocus, could reach up to eat the leaves at the top of very tall trees. Others, like Microraptor, were as small as a bird!

This gigantic beast is **Diplodocus.**

Diplodocus had the **longest tail** of all the dinosaurs, up to **13 m in length**. That's longer than a school bus!

Diplodocus weighed **20,000 kg** and was **26 m long** – that's the length of a **tennis court**!

The **biggest fossilised dinosaur bone** discovered is a thigh bone from a sauropod. It was found in Argentina and was **2.4 m long**! This one bone is taller than the tallest basketball player!

Mamenchisaurus [mah-men-chi-sore-us] was a **sauropod** with a **very long neck**. It was **9 m long**. A **giraffe**'s neck is just **under 2 m**.

This little feathered dinosaur is **Microraptor**, pronounced MIKE-row-rap-tor.

Another sauropod, **Sauroposeidon** [Sore-o-po-sy-don] had the **longest neck** at **12 m long**. That's about the same length as **10 cars**!

Microraptor was a small feathered, winged dinosaur. Its wingspan was only a bit wider than a **pigeon's**! It lived on a diet of **insects** and may have glided between trees hunting for them.

Theropods were meat-eaters that walked on two legs. The most famous of all, **Tyrannosaurus rex**, had short arms for its body size. It measured **12 m long** but its **arms** were only **a metre in length**. Each arm was about the size of a five-year-old!

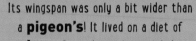

Pentaceratops [pent-ah-ker-ah-tops] had one of the **biggest dinosaur heads** - about **3 m long**. That's as long as an **African elephant** is tall!

Giganotosaurus was one of the **biggest meat-eaters**. It was a terrifying **13 m long**. That's as long as **one-and-a-half buses**!

Stegosaurus was the **size of a van** but it had the **smallest brain** of all the dinosaurs - about the size of a **walnut**.

HOW DID THE DINOSAURS LIVE?

We will never really know everything about dinosaur life but their **fossilised remains** can give us some clues. Scientists have to carefully chip away at the rock surrounding the fossil before they can investigate what dinosaur it came from, what it looked like, what it ate and how it lived.

A large number of fossilised dinosaur eggs and nests have been found. Dinosaurs, like some reptiles today, laid eggs, which came in all shapes and sizes. Some dinosaurs probably laid their eggs and left them to **hatch**. Other dinosaurs may have **looked after** their eggs and babies once they were born (see pages 92–117).

Bone beds that reveal huge numbers of fossilised dinosaur bones can shed some light, and certainly get scientists asking questions about the **lives of dinosaurs**. How did so many dinosaurs end up in one place? Was it a herd of dinosaurs that became trapped and died? Was there a drought in the area?

Fossilised poo can offer a big **insight** into the diet of a dinosaur. **T. rex dung** has been found with the bones of its victim still intact!

This dinosaur is **Maiasaura**, pronounced my-ah-SORE-ah. Its name means 'good mother lizard'.

Maiasaura lived during the Late Cretaceous period in **enormous herds** - adults, juveniles and hatchlings all together. This offered **protection** from meat-eaters like **Troodon** [TROH-oh-don].

Maiasaura is often seen as one of the most **nurturing** dinosaurs as it is thought that it **stayed with its young** when they hatched.

Fossil finds show Maiasaura laid between **30 and 40 eggs** at a time.

It's possible the **eggs** were kept **warm** by using old **plant material** in the **nest**.

A female **Orodromeus** [or-oh-DROM-ee-us] laid about **12 eggs in a spiral**. When they hatched, the hatchlings were almost as fully developed as adults and could leave the nest and feed themselves.

A fossil of a nesting **Oviraptor** [OH-vee-RAP-tor] was discovered with two Velociraptor skulls nearby. Was this Oviraptor protecting its eggs?

BETTER TOGETHER

Some dinosaurs lived in **herds** or **groups**. This would have helped plant-eaters keep an eye out for predators. Meat-eaters could work together to take down larger prey, too.

This long-necked beast is **Puertasaurus**, pronounced PWER-tah-sore-us. Its name means Puerta's lizard.

Many animals today, such as zebra, live together in groups for **protection**. Scientists think some plant-eating **sauropods** lived in **herds**, too. **There was safety in numbers!**

Puertasaurus was about **38 m long**. That's the same as **three-and-a-half buses**!

Fossil finds tell us that **Corythosaurus** [koh-rith-OH-sore-us] had a **hollow crest** on its head. It may have used it to make a **noise**, like a trumpet, to **warn the herd of danger**.

Plant-eating **Tenontosaurus** [ten-ON-toe-sore-us] was one of the most common dinosaurs of the Cretaceous period. A **herd** was probably made up of many dinosaurs living together for **protection**. They could swing their very long tail at predators during an attack. Their tail was half their total 7-m body length!

While many **meat-eaters** hunted or scavenged alone, some, such as Deinonychus [die-NON-i-kuss], might have **hunted in packs**, like **lions** (see pages 70-71).

Deinonychus had **well-developed senses** of sight and hearing, which were vital for communication when working as a pack.

Deinonychus's name means terrible claw.

25

ATTACK

Meat-eating dinosaurs needed to **hunt** or **scavenge** food to survive. These **predators** had characteristics that made them excellent hunters.

Super senses such as excellent eyesight and a keen sense of smell helped meat-eaters **track down** their prey.

Meat-eaters had the **biggest brains** of the dinosaurs. This may have meant they were intelligent hunters. but many factors can cause increased brain size – including the processing power needed for keen eyesight.

Meat-eaters' **skin** probably mimicked the colour of their surroundings to allow them to **hide unseen** by their prey and strike when ready.

This impressive dinosaur is **Allosaurus**.

Hunters needed **sharp teeth** and **claws** to catch their prey. **Allosaurus** teeth were up to **10 cm** long. This is quite small compared to **T. rex** teeth, which were **23 cm long**!

DEFENCE

Most dinosaurs were **plant-eaters**. Many were also a meat-eater's **prey**. They had all sorts of special features that protected them during an attack.

A sauropod's size was its best defence. Plant-eating **Barosaurus** [BAR-oh-sore-us] would have reached the top of a five-storey building when on its back legs.

Many plant-eating dinosaurs had **whip-like tails** to strike their attackers. Some even had extra spikes or clubs, such as **Ankylosaurus** [an-KIE-loh-sore-us]. One blow from its tail could disable even the biggest of meat-eaters.

Their **skin colour** might have helped them **blend into the background**.

Tough skin protected prey from a predator's sharp teeth.

This spiky dinosaur is **Stegosaurus.**

Spines, scutes and **bony plates** all over their body protected many dinosaurs from a meat-eater's sharp teeth and strong jaws. **Scelidosaurus** [skel-EYE-doh-sore-us] was covered in bony plates, called scutes. The scutes were strong enough to snap a predator's teeth!

Stegosaurus had **spikes** at the end of its tail. Fossil finds of these tail spikes are often damaged, suggesting they may have been harmed during an **attack** (see pages 160-161).

THE END OF THE DINOSAURS

65 mya, dinosaurs **disappeared** from the face of the Earth. What happened to them? There are a number of theories but no one is really sure.

Towards the end of the Cretaceous period, volcanoes were erupting more and more frequently. It's possible a series of **volcanic eruptions** sent so much dust and ash into the air it **blocked out sunlight** on Earth. All animals need sunlight. Without sunlight, there wouldn't have been any plants, so no food for the plant-eaters and once they died out, no food for the carnivores.

Or could **climate change** be to blame? Did too much carbon dioxide build up and prevent the Sun's heat from escaping? This might have made Earth **too hot** to sustain life.

Some scientists have even suggested dinosaur bodies were becoming **too big for their brains**, and so many dinosaurs couldn't compete with faster-thinking animals.

Earth has always been hit by rocks and debris from space. Most burn up in Earth's atmosphere but some can get through. The most accepted theory is that a **meteorite** hit Earth and destroyed the dinosaurs. In 1991, scientists found evidence of a **huge crater** in Mexico. Could this have been where the meteorite landed?

It could even be possible that a **tsunami** spread across the land, destroying habitats, plants and animals.

One of the more bizarre theories is that **small mammals** ate so many dinosaur eggs that the dinosaur population could no longer renew itself so it died out!

HOW DO WE KNOW ABOUT THE DINOSAURS?

Fossils of dinosaurs tell us how large an animal was, what it ate and how it died. A fossil forms when an animal or plant is buried under mud and sand over millions of years.

In some parts of the world, **'dinosaur traps'** reveal lots of dinosaurs died together in one place. Dinosaur fossils have been found on every continent on Earth! Here are some of their locations.

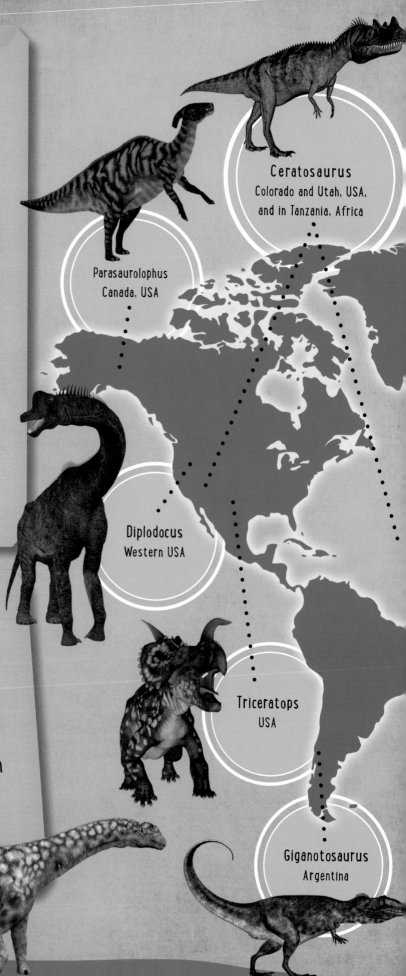

Ceratosaurus
Colorado and Utah, USA, and in Tanzania, Africa

Parasaurolophus
Canada, USA

Diplodocus
Western USA

Triceratops
USA

Giganotosaurus
Argentina

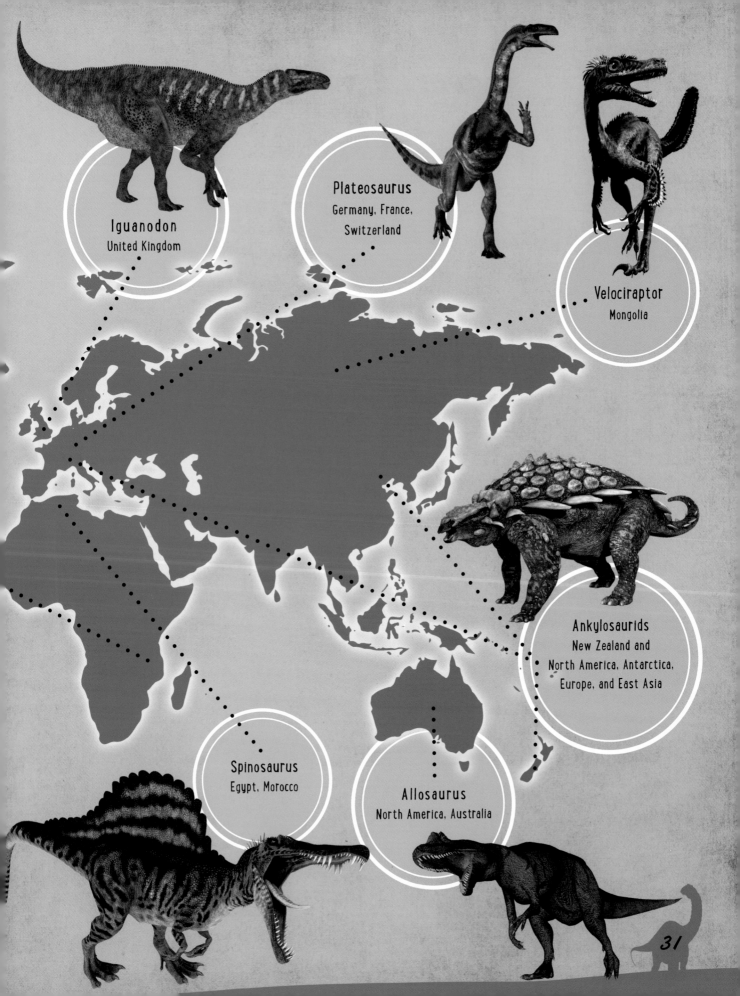

Iguanodon
United Kingdom

Plateosaurus
Germany, France,
Switzerland

Velociraptor
Mongolia

Ankylosaurids
New Zealand and
North America, Antarctica,
Europe, and East Asia

Spinosaurus
Egypt, Morocco

Allosaurus
North America, Australia

31

DINOSAURS TODAY

The best place to find out about dinosaurs is at your nearest **natural history museum**. You can also look up in the sky ... Did you know that modern birds are the descendants of dinosaurs?

Not all creatures died out with the dinosaurs. It's possible to find examples of prehistoric life all around us today. Modern-day **crocodiles**, **sharks** and **jellyfish** have barely changed from the time of the dinosaurs.

The discovery of **'dino-birds'**, such as **Sinosauropteryx** [sine-oh-sore-OP-ter-iks] and **Archaeopteryx** [ark-ee-OPT-er-ix], has led scientists to think that **dinosaurs are related to birds**.

Some **modern birds** still have **clawed wings** like some dinosaurs. **Hoatzin chicks** have two tiny claws on each wing tip.

QUICK DINO FACTS

TROODON

LENGTH: 2 m

WEIGHT: 40 kg

DIET: Small mammals and reptiles

LIVED: Late Cretaceous period

FIRST FOSSIL DISCOVERY Montana, USA in 1855

FACT: Troodon had the largest brain of any dinosaur, relative to its body size.

STEGOSAURUS

LENGTH: 6–9 m

WEIGHT: 2,400 kg

DIET: Plants

LIVED: Late Jurassic period

FIRST FOSSIL DISCOVERY: Colorado, USA in 1903

FACT: Stegosaurus' bony plates may have blushed red when blood rushed to them!

COMPSOGNATHUS

LENGTH: 65 cm

WEIGHT: 3.6 kg

DIET: Lizards

LIVED: Jurassic period

FIRST FOSSIL DISCOVERY: Bavaria, Germany, 1859

FACT: Compsognathus was only the size of a chicken, but it was still a fierce predator.

SAUROPOSEIDON

LENGTH: 30 m

WEIGHT: 60,000 kg

DIET: Plants

LIVED: Cretaceous period

FIRST FOSSIL DISCOVERY: Oklahoma, USA in 1999

FACT: Reached 18 m high. It could easily peer into a six-storey window!

GIGANTIC
PLANT-EATERS

GENTLE DINOSAURS

When we think of dinosaurs we often think of mean killing machines, but in fact more than half of all dinosaurs were **herbivores**. This means they ate **plants**. Plant-eaters, such as Triceratops, were hunted and eaten by meat-eaters, such as Tyrannosaurus rex.

Some plant-eaters were so **big** they had to eat the **weight** of a **small car** in plants every day!

Conifers were **everywhere** during the Mesozoic Era. They made up a large part of a plant-eater's **diet**.

Today, there are 12,000 species of **fern**. For every living type of fern, scientists think there are **nine more fossil species**. That's **108,000 species of fern**. No wonder dinosaurs like Stegosaurus loved them!

Not all plant-eating dinosaurs had the right kind of **teeth** for chewing their food. Some dinosaurs **swallowed** plant food in **one big gulp**. The **bacteria** in their **stomachs** helped break down their lunch!

Plant-eaters came in all shapes and sizes. **Long-necked** dinosaurs could reach high up into trees to eat tall leaves and branches. **Short-necked** herbivores grazed on low-lying plants.

CHAIN

Tyrannosaurus rex

Triceratops

FOOD

Plant-eaters like **Styracosaurus** ate so much that scientists think they wore their **teeth** down very quickly. Many had teeth arranged in groups called **batteries**. Older teeth on top were constantly replaced by **new teeth** underneath.

palm fronds

Styracosaurus
[sty-RAK-oh-sore-us]

TINY AND TALL

There were **different kinds** of plant-eating dinosaurs; some were **big** and some were **small**. Some walked on **two legs** and others got about on **four**. Some swallowed their food whole, while others chewed their lunch!

This spiky beast is a **Gargoyleosaurus**, pronounced **gahr-GOY-lee-oh-sore-us**. Its name means gargoyle lizard.

Gargoyleosaurus was quite **small** - only about 4 m long - but could still weigh as much as 900 kg. That's about the weight of **two polar bears**!

Micropachycephalosaurus [MIKE-row-PAK-ee-KEFF-ah-loh-sore-us] was a small **rabbit-sized** dinosaur that walked on two legs!

Aquilops [ah-QUILL-ops] was a **tiny** plant-eater that was the size of a **small cat**. It weighed **1.6 kg** and was only **60 cm long**.

Camptosaurus was a Jurassic dinosaur that was only about **1 m tall** but it could **stand up** on two legs to reach food higher up. This plant-eater could run away from predators at a **speed** of up to **25 kilometres per hour**. That's as fast as a **wild turkey**!

Pronounced, **KAMP-toe-sore-us**, its name means bent lizard.

Brachiosaurus was one of the **largest plant-eaters** that ever lived. This giant was **15 m high** – that's **three giraffes** tall – and **30 m long**. Its neck alone was **9 m long**!

Brachiosaurus means arm lizard.

Nigersaurus [NEE-zhayr-sore-us], a plant-eater from the Early Cretaceous period, had as many as **1,000 teeth**! Experts think it may have grown a new set of teeth every 15 days.

GRAZING GIANTS

Sauropods were a group of plant-eating dinosaurs. They were the **longest**, **heaviest** and **tallest** animals to ever walk the Earth. They usually walked slowly on four column-shaped legs.

This dinosaur is called Camarasaurus, pronounced **KAM-ar-a-sore-us**. The name means chambered lizard.

Sauropods had long necks and tails, small heads and blunt teeth. Because of their size, sauropods would have had to eat almost all of the time!

Scientists can't be certain if sauropods like **Apatosaurus** could hold their **giant necks** up high. To be able to **pump blood** all the way up its long neck, the dinosaur's **heart** alone would have had to weigh **4,000 kg**. That's **15 times heavier** than one side of the heart of a **fin whale**!

Sauropods were **tall** and **heavy**! Did these giants have a clever way of lightening their load? **Fossil bones** have been found with small pockets of air, called **air sacs**, inside them. These air sacs might have helped to **lighten** the weight of the skeletons of these big dinosaurs.

Brachiosaurus

Cetiosauriscus

Mamenchisaurus

NORTH AMERICA

EUROPE

ASIA

Argentinosaurus

AFRICA

AUSTRALIA

SOUTH AMERICA

Nigersaurus

Rhoetosaurus

Sauropod fossils have been found on every continent except Antarctica.

Sauropods may have been big but they had small heads and tiny brains. For example, Ampelosaurus' [AM-pel-oh-sore-us] brain was only the size of one-and-a-half walnuts!

Sauropod **skeletons** have been found with **necks** up to **15 m long**. That's six times longer than the current record holder – the **giraffe**!

x 6

Camarasaurus had very **large teeth** for a sauropod. Each one was shaped like a **chisel**, and very strong, so it could eat **tougher plant** material than other sauropods such as Diplodocus.

Some plant-eaters swallowed **rocks** called **gastroliths**. These helped break down the **food** in the dinosaur's **stomach**.

gastrolith

DINO DEFENCE

Plant-eating dinosaurs were always on the look out for **predators**. They didn't want to end up as a meat-eater's lunch! Scientists think plant-eaters had **tough**, **leathery skin** to **protect** from razor-sharp, meat-eating teeth. Some dinosaurs also had **horns**, **spikes** and **tail clubs** to defend themselves.

Thick-skulled dinosaurs like **Stegoceras** [ste-GOS-er-as] might have used their **heads** to head butt one another during **fights** over a mate!

Ankylosaurus was covered in body armour similar to an **armadillo's** today.

Kentrosaurus had long, bony **spikes** running in pairs down its back and tail for **protection**. It could swing its tail at an attacker with enough force to fracture a human skull!

Pronounced **ken-TROH-sore-us**, its name means spiky lizard.

Centrosaurus' head was built for **defence**. It had a **bony frill** to protect its neck, two **large horns** on top of the frill and a pair of **small horns** over its eyes. It also had a horn on its nose, like a **rhinoceros**.

Pronounced **Cen-TROH-sore-us**, its name means sharp pointed lizard.

Size was often a plant-eating dinosaur's **biggest defence**. Only fierce, hungry **predators** and packs of meat-eating dinosaurs, such as Deinonychus [die-NON-i-kuss], would have dared take on some of these gigantic beasts.

Apatosaurus means deceptive lizard.

Apatosaurus may have used its long **tail** to **strike** at its enemies.

Apatosaurus wasn't a defenceless plant-eater. Its **height**, **whip-like tail** and **clawed feet** meant it could have put up quite a **fight** with any of the biggest predators it lived alongside. The predator **Allosaurus** [AL-oh-saw-russ] wouldn't even have been able to reach Apatosaurus' neck during an attack!

43

SAUROPOD HERDS

We've learned that scientists think some plant-eating dinosaurs lived in **herds** or **family groups**. There is evidence that even some of the **largest dinosaurs** to ever walk the Earth – the **sauropods** – lived in groups.

Alamosaurus, pronounced **ah-la-mow-SORE-us**, means Alamo lizard.

Some herds of sauropods may have **migrated** long distances in search of food. This is because they were so big that they needed to eat the weight of a small car in plants every day!

Fossilised footprints in Texas, USA, might have been made by **23 sauropods**. The different footprint sizes may reveal that the **adults led their young** across land, possibly walking long distances to find food.

Scientists have found bone beds with groups of **dinosaur bones**. How did they all get there? Perhaps these dinosaurs were living in a herd and became **trapped in mud**, caught up in a **flood** or they died because of **droughts** in the area.

Alamosaurus fossil finds suggest that **juvenile** dinosaurs may have **stuck together**. This may have been down to **size**, as they might have had different **dietary needs** from adult dinosaurs. Living together would have given them greater **protection** from predators, too.

The largest sauropods weighed ten times more than an elephant. To see these creatures in a herd would have been quite a sight!

Fossilised trackways reveal where dinosaurs might have walked. Some **herds** could have been made up of **hundreds** of individuals.

THE HEAVIEST SAUROPOD

Argentinosaurus was an **enormous sauropod**! It was **35 m long** and weighed in at **70,000 kg**. This giant lived during the **Cretaceous** period.

Argentinosaurus' name means Argentina lizard.

Argentinosaurus may have been **preyed** on by the biggest meat-eater of the time – **Giganotosaurus**.

Argentinosaurus carried its weight on four huge column-shaped legs.

This massive dinosaur probably got rid of **15 litres of poo** at a time!

Argentinosaurus fed on **leaves** at the top of tall trees, using its long **neck** to reach up **high**. It used its teeth for chewing and grinding its food.

Argentinosaurus may have continued to **grow** throughout its **entire life**. It may have taken as long as **40 years** to reach its **adult size**!

Argentinosaurus may have lived in **herds** to **protect** its **eggs** and young from predator **attack**.

One Argentinosaurus **vertebra** was about **1.5 m tall**. This is almost the same height as the biggest jump a **red kangaroo** can do!

Its weight meant Argentinosaurus moved at about **8 kph** - as fast as a **tortoise**.

An Argentinosaurus **egg** was about 20 cm wide – the size of a **basketball**.

SAILS AND SPINES

Amargasaurus was a bizarre-looking **Early Cretaceous** dinosaur that, at **12 m long**, was the length of one-and-a-half buses. Amargasaurus had two rows of **spines** that may have joined together to form a **sail** running down the length of its back.

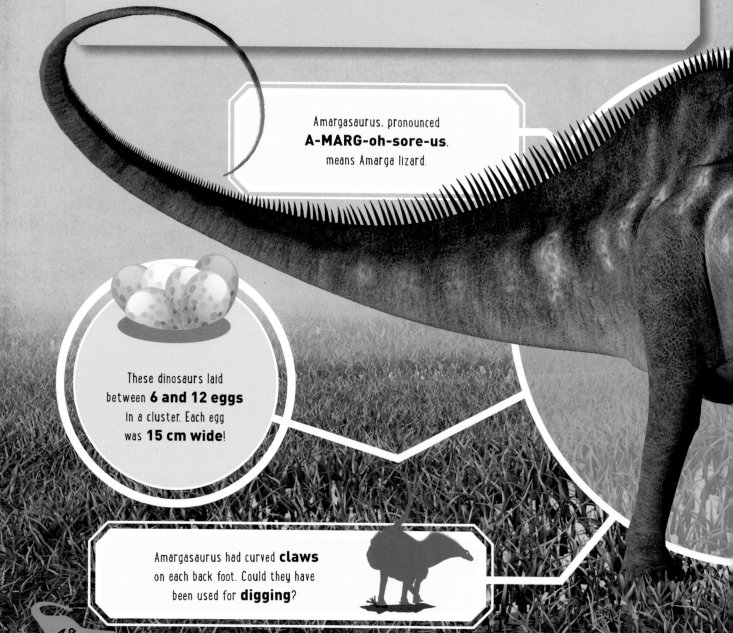

Amargasaurus, pronounced **A-MARG-oh-sore-us**, means Amarga lizard.

These dinosaurs laid between **6 and 12 eggs** in a cluster. Each egg was **15 cm wide**!

Amargasaurus had curved **claws** on each back foot. Could they have been used for **digging**?

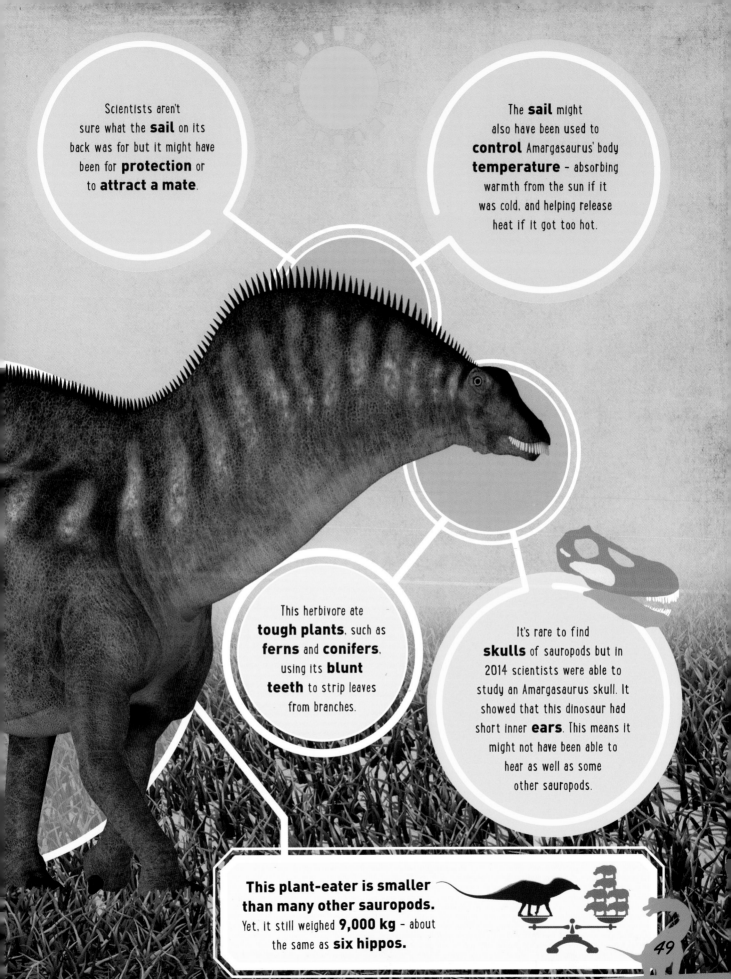

Scientists aren't sure what the **sail** on its back was for but it might have been for **protection** or to **attract a mate**.

The **sail** might also have been used to **control** Amargasaurus' body **temperature** - absorbing warmth from the sun if it was cold, and helping release heat if it got too hot.

This herbivore ate **tough plants**, such as **ferns** and **conifers**, using its **blunt teeth** to strip leaves from branches.

It's rare to find **skulls** of sauropods but in 2014 scientists were able to study an Amargasaurus skull. It showed that this dinosaur had short inner **ears**. This means it might not have been able to hear as well as some other sauropods.

This plant-eater is smaller than many other sauropods. Yet, it still weighed **9,000 kg** - about the same as **six hippos**.

DOUBLE BEAM GIANT

Diplodocus lived during the **Late Jurassic** period and is one of the **longest** animals that ever roamed the Earth.

Diplodocus means double beam.

Diplodocus' **tail** was long and strong, and may have been used as a **balance**, allowing it to rear up on its back legs to reach food that was very high up.

Diplodocus' **long tail** might have been used as a **whip** during a predator **attack**. The tail weighed **1,590 kg** so would have sounded as loud as cannon fire!

Diplodocus **poo** would have dropped from a great height. On the ground it may have formed a pool about **10 m wide** – yuck!

For a dinosaur as big as Diplodocus, its **eggs** were quite **small** – only 1.5 kg. Scientists think this made the eggs in the nest vulnerable to fewer predators as they were able to **hatch** into baby dinosaurs more **quickly**.

At 26 m long Diplodocus was the same length as three school buses!

Diplodocus weighed up to 25,000 kg – as much as a full concrete mixer!

This dinosaur's **neck** and tail was made up of almost **100 vertebrae**.

This giant plant-eater had rows of **teeth** like a **comb** that it used to strip the leaves from plants and swallow whole.

Diplodocus lived at the same time as some of the fiercest meat-eating dinosaurs, such as Allosaurus and Ceratosaurus [Keh-RAT-oh-sore-us]. Luckily, Diplodocus' **giant size** probably meant it was **safe** from most **predators**.

Diplodocus probably didn't **sleep** for any long periods of time. It's thought it **constantly ate**, **walked** and **slept** throughout the day and night.

BONES AND PLATES

Stegosaurus was a **large**, slow-moving plant-eater. It had **17 bony plates** on its back, buried within its skin, which might have helped keep the dinosaur **cool**. The plates might have **protected** the dinosaur from **predator attack** or even been used in **mating displays**. Scientists aren't sure!

Stegosaurus means roof lizard.

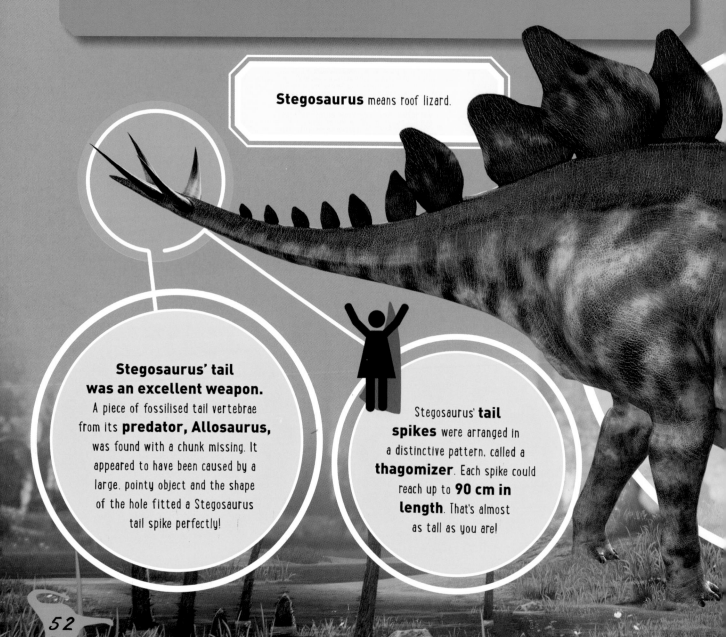

Stegosaurus' tail was an excellent weapon. A piece of fossilised tail vertebrae from its **predator, Allosaurus,** was found with a chunk missing. It appeared to have been caused by a large, pointy object and the shape of the hole fitted a Stegosaurus tail spike perfectly!

Stegosaurus' **tail spikes** were arranged in a distinctive pattern, called a **thagomizer**. Each spike could reach up to **90 cm in length**. That's almost as tall as you are!

At 3,000 kg, Stegosaurus was twice as heavy as a car.

Stegosaurus was a slow mover. Its short front legs and longer back legs meant it couldn't walk faster than about **7 kph**. That's only a little bit faster than the walking speed of a human adult!

Stegosaurus' mouth was shaped like a bird's and its small **teeth**, called 'cheek teeth', chewed plants. It also swallowed **gastroliths** to help digest its food.

Stegosaurus might have been big but its **brain** was only the size of a **plum**!

THREE-HORNED HEAD

One of the most famous dinosaurs is Triceratops. This plant-eater, with its **three horns**, parrot-like **beak** and large **frill**, is one of the largest and most striking dinosaurs to have ever lived.

Triceratops means three-horned face.

Triceratops might have **charged** when threatened, just like a **rhino** charges today.

A baby Triceratops' **head** was about the same size as a human head. But palaeontologists have discovered adult Triceratops **skulls** that are over 2 m long!

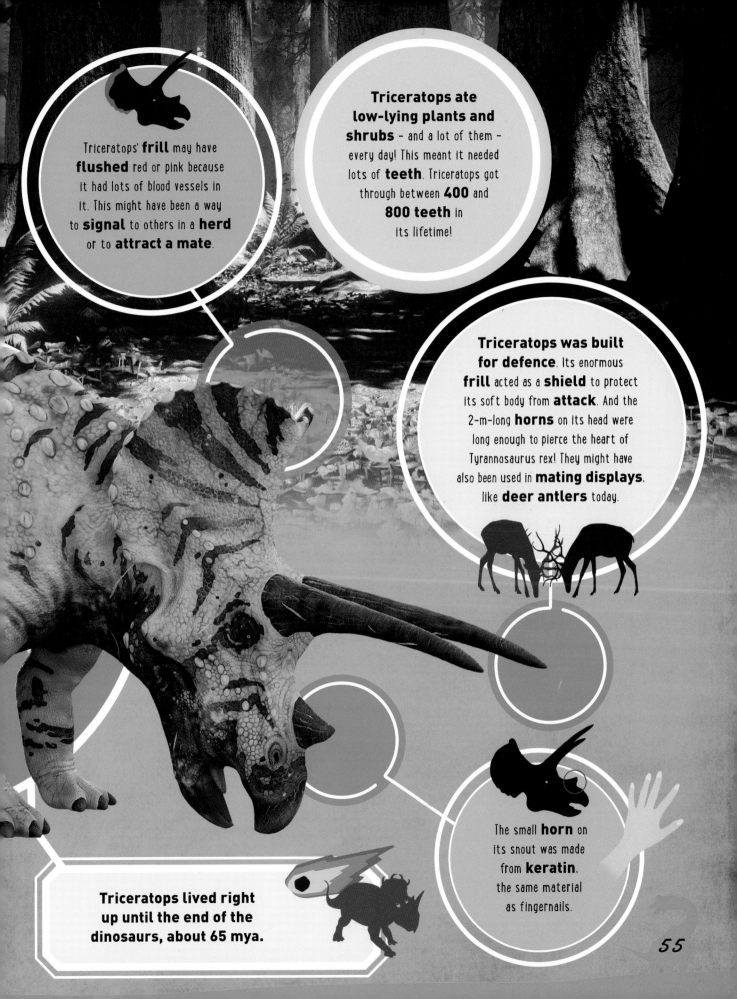

Triceratops' **frill** may have **flushed** red or pink because it had lots of blood vessels in it. This might have been a way to **signal** to others in a **herd** or to **attract a mate**.

Triceratops ate low-lying plants and shrubs – and a lot of them – every day! This meant it needed lots of **teeth**. Triceratops got through between **400** and **800 teeth** in its lifetime!

Triceratops was built for defence. Its enormous **frill** acted as a **shield** to protect its soft body from **attack**. And the 2-m-long **horns** on its head were long enough to pierce the heart of Tyrannosaurus rex! They might have also been used in **mating displays**, like **deer antlers** today.

The small **horn** on its snout was made from **keratin**, the same material as fingernails.

Triceratops lived right up until the end of the dinosaurs, about 65 mya.

SUIT OF ARMOUR

Ankylosaurus was a plant-eater that was **protected** from head to toe with **bony plates** and **spikes**. It was almost as wide as it was long. A meat-eater would have had to be really hungry to attack this amoured dinosaur!

Ankylosaurus' **tail club** was made of **fused bone.** This is when the bones are joined together to form one big mass of bone. The tail club was so strong it could **shatter bone** during a fight.

Ankylosaurus didn't chew its food. Breaking down all that food in its **stomach** might have made this dinosaur very **gassy!**

Ankylosaurus' size meant that it ate a lot every day! It would strip the leaves from branches as it moved slowly through its habitat at about **10 kph.** That's only a bit faster than a lumbering elephant.

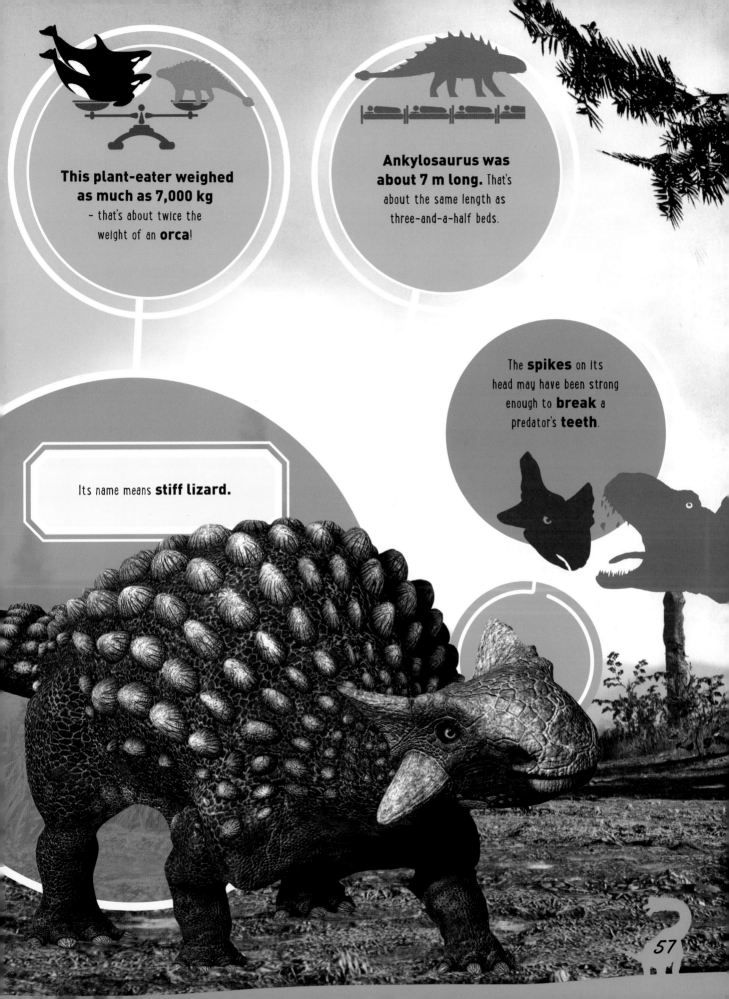

This plant-eater weighed as much as 7,000 kg – that's about twice the weight of an **orca**!

Ankylosaurus was about 7 m long. That's about the same length as three-and-a-half beds.

The **spikes** on its head may have been strong enough to **break** a predator's **teeth**.

Its name means **stiff lizard.**

CLAWED CREATURE

Iguanodon was a plant-eating dinosaur that lived during the **Early Cretaceous** period. It was first discovered in **Sussex**, **UK** but fossils have since been found in other parts of **Europe**, **Africa** and **North America**.

Iguanodon moved at 24 kph. That's the same speed as a charging bull!

Scientists have found several **fossils** from different Iguanodons together in the same place. This could mean these dinosaurs **lived in groups for protection.**

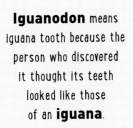

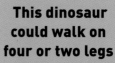

Iguanodon means iguana tooth because the person who discovered it thought its teeth looked like those of an **iguana**.

When Iguanodon was first **discovered**, some scientists didn't think the bones belonged to a dinosaur. They were dismissed as **fish teeth** or the teeth of a **rhinoceros**!

This dinosaur could walk on four or two legs – whatever it fancied!

Iguanodon had large **thumb claws** for **self-defence** and **flexible fingers**, possibly for **foraging** for food.

Iguanodon had **three short, thick toes** on its back feet. These might have been **padded** to allow this huge dinosaur to evenly spread its weight across its feet and walk more comfortably.

This plant-eater may have had **bendy fingers** to hold its food and possibly break open seeds and fruit.

QUICK PLANT-EATER FACTS

Plant-eating dinosaurs were some of the strangest creatures to ever walk the Earth. Check out these fascinating dino facts!

PARASAUROLOPHUS

HEIGHT: 2.8 m

LENGTH: 11 m

WEIGHT: 3,500 kg

LIVED: Late Cretaceous

LOCATION: Canada, USA

FIRST FOSSIL DISCOVERY: Alberta, Canada 1922

FACT: Parasaurolophus may have used its curved crest to make a noise to warn other members of its herd of danger.

GALLIMIMUS

HEIGHT: 1.9 m

LENGTH: 6 m

WEIGHT: 200 kg

LIVED: Late Cretaceous

LOCATION: Mongolia

FIRST FOSSIL DISCOVERY: Gobi Desert, Mongolia, 1972

FACT: Gallimimus was one of the fastest dinosaurs. At 70 kph, it could run as fast as an ostrich!

LESOTHOSAURUS

HEIGHT: 0.5 m

LENGTH: 1 m

WEIGHT: 10 kg

LIVED: Late Jurassic

LOCATION: Lesotho

FIRST FOSSIL DISCOVERY: Lesotho, 1978

FACT: This early dinosaur had five-fingered hands!

NOTHRONYCHUS

HEIGHT: Unknown

LENGTH: 5.3 m

WEIGHT: 900 kg

LIVED: Late Cretaceous

LOCATION: USA

FIRST FOSSIL DISCOVERY: New Mexico, USA, 2001

FACT: This strange dinosaur may have evolved from a meat-eater to a plant-eater.

STYGIMOLOCH

HEIGHT: 1.3 m

LENGTH: 3 m

WEIGHT: 200 kg

LIVED: Late Cretaceous

LOCATION: USA

FIRST FOSSIL DISCOVERY: First discovered in the 1800s. Named in 1983, Montana, USA

FACT: Stygimoloch had a ring of horns around its skull. Some people think it looks a bit like a devil!

MINMI

HEIGHT: 0.9 m

LENGTH: 3 m

WEIGHT: 450 kg

LIVED: Early Cretaceous

LOCATION: Australia

FIRST FOSSIL DISCOVERY: Queensland, Australia, 1964

FACT: This dinosaur was named after Minmi Crossing in Queensland, Australia.

KILLER
DINOSAURS

DEADLY HUNTERS

Meat-eating dinosaurs – the **carnivores** – were killing machines! Most were theropods that came in all shapes and sizes, from enormous beasts, such as **Tyrannosaurus rex** and **Allosaurus**, to teeny-tiny dinosaurs like **Microraptor**.

This mighty meat-eater is **Tyrannosaurus rex.** Its name means tyrant lizard king.

Hesperonychus [hes-puh-ruh-NIE-kuss] was a **tiny** meat-eater that weighed no more than a **chicken**!

Many meat-eaters walked on two feet. This made them **fast** and meant they could catch their prey with their clawed hands.

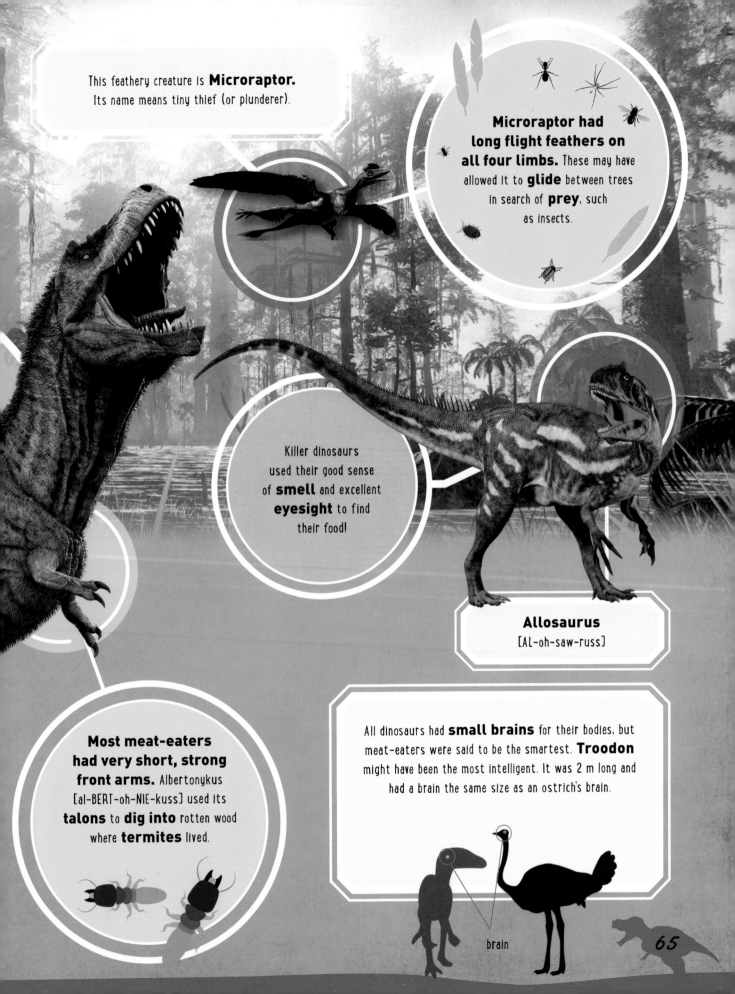

This feathery creature is **Microraptor.** Its name means tiny thief (or plunderer).

Microraptor had long flight feathers on all four limbs. These may have allowed it to **glide** between trees in search of **prey**, such as insects.

Killer dinosaurs used their good sense of **smell** and excellent **eyesight** to find their food!

Allosaurus
[AL-oh-saw-russ]

Most meat-eaters had very short, strong front arms. Albertonykus [al-BERT-oh-NIE-kuss] used its **talons** to **dig into** rotten wood where **termites** lived.

All dinosaurs had **small brains** for their bodies, but meat-eaters were said to be the smartest. **Troodon** might have been the most intelligent. It was 2 m long and had a brain the same size as an ostrich's brain.

brain

65

BUILT TO KILL

Meat-eating dinosaurs had to **hunt** or **scavenge** to stay alive. They were **made for speed** with strong hind legs to chase down their prey.

Many killer dinosaurs had long **tails**, which they held horizontally, to **balance** out their strong necks, big heads and powerful jaws.

Scientists don't know for sure, but a meat-eater's **skin** or **feathers** probably helped it **blend in** with its surroundings when on the hunt for food.

Some meat-eaters may have been **nocturnal hunters**. Troodon had big, cat-like **eyes** that could seek out prey in the darkness.

Like **sharks** and **crocodiles**, most meat-eating dinosaurs would **grow** a new **tooth** to replace any that fell out or broke.

Tyrannosaurus rex had over 50 teeth! Each one was **23 cm long** – about the size of a banana!

Killer dinosaurs had powerful jaws that snapped shut like a **crocodile**. They also had **sharp teeth** that could cut through flesh and bone.

Some paleontologists think that even though T. rex had **short arms,** it might still have been able to grasp **up to 397 lbs.** of prey. Their arms were very strong and could move in all directions, so they could have pulled prey in close for biting. That's like being able to hold on to a **gorilla**!

This beast is **Saurophaganax**, pronounced **sore-oh-fag-ah-naks**. Its name means king of the lizard eaters.

DINOSAUR DINNERS

All dinosaurs were part of a **food chain**. There were lots of **plants** to feed the **plant-eaters** at the bottom of the food chain. These plant-eaters were then gobbled up by the **meat-eaters**.

Some meat-eating dinosaurs may have also been **scavengers**. A scavenger is an animal that finds and eats the **carcass** of other dinosaurs, rather than hunting for its next meal.

Not all meat-eating dinosaurs hunted other dinosaurs. **Some of them ate fish, insects, eggs and mammals.** The teeth of some dinosaurs, such as Gallimimus [gal-lee-MEEM-us], were adapted to eat both meat and plants.

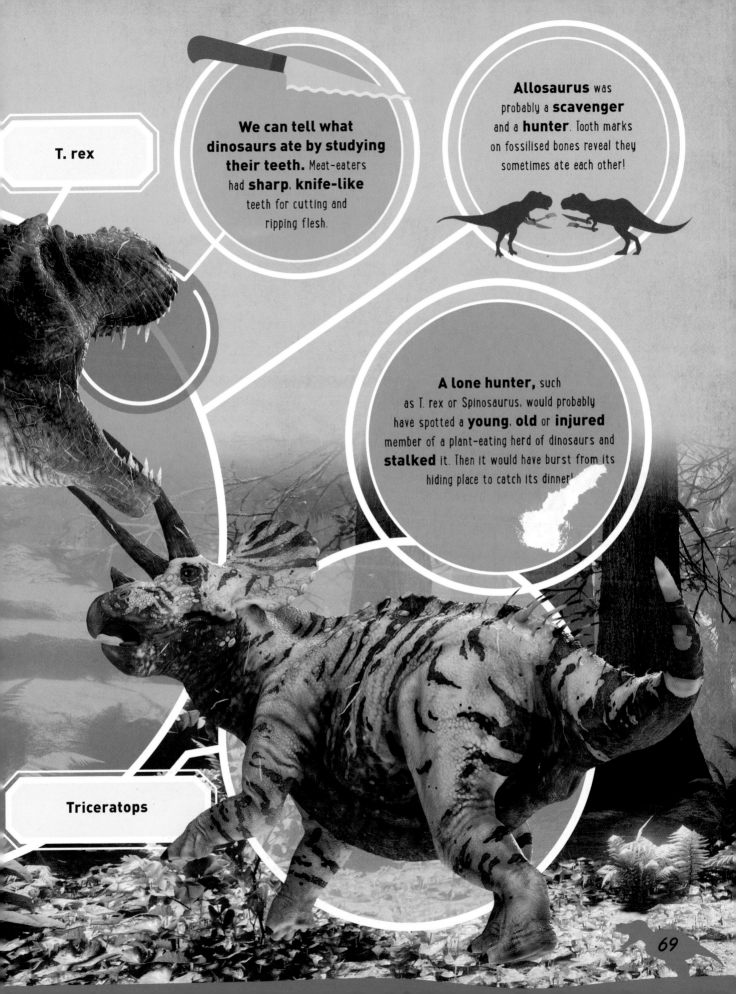

T. rex

We can tell what dinosaurs ate by studying their teeth. Meat-eaters had **sharp, knife-like** teeth for cutting and ripping flesh.

Allosaurus was probably a **scavenger** and a **hunter**. Tooth marks on fossilised bones reveal they sometimes ate each other!

A lone hunter, such as T. rex or Spinosaurus, would probably have spotted a **young, old** or **injured** member of a plant-eating herd of dinosaurs and **stalked** it. Then it would have burst from its hiding place to catch its dinner!

Triceratops

DINO GANGS

Scientists also think some meat-eaters **hunted in packs**, like wolves and hyenas do today. They used their intelligence to **work together** and catch prey that was much bigger than them.

Deinonychus is one dinosaur that probably hunted in groups. It may have **attacked** prey much larger than itself, like **Tenontosaurus.** The group might have held down their prey with their strong legs and claws, and possibly even started eating it while it was still alive!

Tenontosaurus

Eoraptor was one of the earliest pack-hunting dinosaurs. It had **eyes** on the side of its head for **all-round vision**.

The pack-hunting **Megaraptor** [meg-a-RAP-tor] was a meat-eating theropod. Each one weighed as much as a **black rhino** and could possibly run as fast as an **ostrich**. Imagine a pack charging towards you!

Utahraptors, pronounced **YOO-tah-RAP-tors**, could take down an Iguanodon. Their name means Utah thief.

In 2014, a huge block of sandstone was pulled from a mountain in Utah, USA. It has been nicknamed the '**death trap**' as six or more meat-eating **Utahraptors** have been found there. Did they die together, **hunting as a pack**?

The discovery of 22 individual **Albertosaurus** [al-BERT-oh-saw-russ] fossils found together suggests that these dinosaurs hunted in packs. The bones were a mix of young and adult Albertosaurus. Some scientists think it's even possible that the younger, faster Albertosaurus **drove prey** towards the jaws of the stronger adult dinosaurs.

TERRIFYING T. REX

Tyrannosaurus rex was one of the **strongest** and **biggest** of the deadly dinosaurs. It lived throughout what is now North America during the last part of the **Cretaceous period**.

T. rex could grow to 12 m in length and 4 m tall. That's more than the length of a double-decker bus but the same height.

New scientific methods have helped scientists to **discover** that T. rex probably had tough, scraggly **feathers** on parts of its body.

It could weigh up to 7,000 kg. That's the same weight as **two hippos**.

In one bite, T. rex could fit 225 kg of meat in its mouth. That's the equivalent of **two-and-a-half sheep** per mouthful!

A T. rex **eyeball** was the same size as a human adult's fist!

The **force** of its **bite** would have felt like the weight of **five small cars** crashing down on whatever it was crunching! This makes T. rex the **hardest-biting** land animal ever known.

T. rex liked to **hunt** large **plant-eaters**, but it was also a **scavenger**, eating already-dead animals.

73

SCARY SPINOSAURUS

Spinosaurus was the **largest** meat-eating dinosaur. It walked the floodplains of **North Africa** looking for its prey. This killer may have **hunted large fish** and **sharks** in the water. It might have even been able to **swim**.

Spinosaurus means thorn lizard.

It was **18 m long** – the length of two buses – and had huge **spines** over its **back**. These spines joined together to form a **sail** about 2 m high. This would have made the beast a frightening **predator**!

Spinosaurus could weigh up to 4,000 kg. That's as much as an **Asian elephant**!

Scientists don't know for sure what the **sail** was used for. It might have helped a male **attract** a female, a bit like a male **peacock** with its tail feathers today.

It's also thought that the **sail** might have been a kind of solar panel, helping Spinosaurus **warm up** quickly in the morning, and keeping it **cool** in the midday sun.

Nostrils

Spinosaurus had the longest head of any meat-eater. It was about 1.8 m long – the same length as a grown man!

Like a **crocodile**, Spinosaurus had a long, narrow snout with **nostrils** in the middle of its skull. This was perfect for **hunting** prey in **water**!

Spinosaurus could stand 6 storeys high!

Spinosaurus may have been able to open its **mouth** extra wide, like a **pelican**. This meant it might have been able to **swallow huge prey** in one **big gulp**!

75

CUTE COELOPHYSIS

In the **Late Triassic** period, a small dinosaur used its **speed** and **agility** to catch tiny reptiles and insects. **Coelophysis** may have only been 3 m long but it was far from cute. This killer had sharp **teeth** and **claws** to hold down and kill its prey.

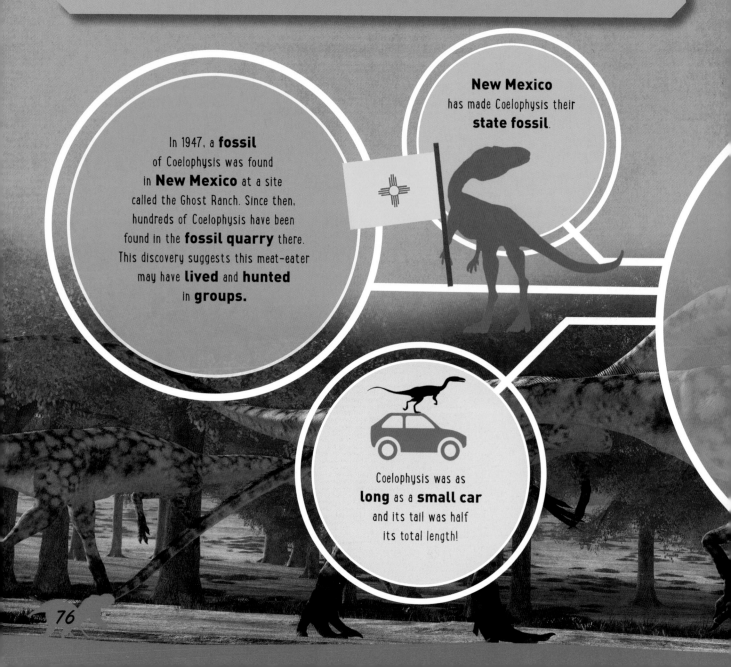

In 1947, a **fossil** of Coelophysis was found in **New Mexico** at a site called the Ghost Ranch. Since then, hundreds of Coelophysis have been found in the **fossil quarry** there. This discovery suggests this meat-eater may have **lived** and **hunted** in **groups**.

New Mexico has made Coelophysis their **state fossil**.

Coelophysis was as **long** as a **small car** and its tail was half its total length!

Coelophysis had **very large eyes**, which would have helped when **hunting**. It may even be a hint that this dinosaur hunted at **night**.

Coelophysis bones have been to space! Astronauts on the Space Shuttle *Endeavour* took a Coelophysis **skull** with them on a mission to the Mir space station in **1998**.

Its name means 'hollow form'. Coelophysis was given this name because it had **hollow bones**. This meant its body was light, which helped it to be a **swift, agile hunter**.

Studies of fossilised Coelophysis remains suggest that this dinosaur laid as many as **25 eggs** at a time.

VICIOUS VELOCIRAPTOR

Velociraptor was a small but mighty meat-eater that lived during the Late Cretaceous period, around **84–80 mya.**

Velociraptor means speedy thief.

Velociraptors had a fine **feather-like covering** that they may have used to keep their eggs **warm** when **nesting**.

Velociraptor had strong back **legs** and could run at speeds of up to **65 kilometres per hour!**

With **27-30 teeth** in its **strong jaws**, Velociraptor had just over half the number of teeth as T. rex. It feasted on **prey** such as **reptiles**, **insects** and **smaller dinosaurs**.

It would use its three-fingered **claws** to grab its prey before ripping its flesh with **razor-sharp teeth.**

Velociraptor was about the **size** of a **sheep** and weighed less than a **turkey**.

Its **deadliest** weapon was a huge **9-cm claw** on each of its feet.

GRUESOME GIGANOTOSAURUS

Giganotosaurus means 'giant southern lizard' and this dinosaur was certainly big! It lived during the **Early Cretaceous** period, about 30 million years before the mighty Tyrannosaurus rex walked the Earth!

Pronounced
gig-an-OH-toe-SORE-us.

Giganotosaurus had a long, narrow tail. It may have helped the dinosaur **turn quickly** when chasing after its prey.

Giganotosaurus could **run** at about **50 kph**. That's as fast as a **car** on a city road.

With its long **chin** and sharp **front teeth**, Giganotosaurus was able to **bite** and **rip** its prey, rather than crushing and crunching it up, like T. rex did.

A Giganotosaurus **brain** was tiny – **the size of a small cucumber**!

Giganotosaurus' **teeth** could grow up to the size of a large **banana**. They had **serrated** edges for slicing through skin and flesh.

This dinosaur could have swallowed a human in one bite!

Each of Giganotosaurus' front **arms** ended in three **fingers**, with three long, curved **claws**, which it used to hold its prey.

This dinosaur could reach up to **13 m in length** and weighed **8,000 kg**, which is only a little bit smaller than **two orcas**. Imagine that running towards you!

GIANT YUTYRANNUS HUALI

In 2012, a giant feathered meat-eater was scientifically named **Yutyrannus huali**. This killer dinosaur was found in China and is the **largest feathered** animal known to have existed.

Yutyrannus was about **9 m long** and weighed **1,300 kg** - about the **weight** of a **small hippo**.

Yutyrannus huali may have used its **feathers** to keep its **nest eggs** warm in the cool habitat it lived in.

Several Yutyrannus hauli **skeletons** have been found in the same location, which could mean this dinosaur **hunted in packs**.

Pronounced **yoo-ti-RAN-us hoo-a-li**, its name is a mix of Mandarin and Latin, and means 'beautiful feathered tyrant'.

Its feathers were up to 20 cm long. The feathers might have helped the dinosaur **blend in** with its habitat of forests and lakes, with cooler winters and possibly snow.

This **Cretaceous** beast lived during the peak of the dinosaurs' time on Earth. It couldn't fly but its simple **downy covering** probably kept it **warm**.

Before the discovery of Yutyrannus, **Beipiaosaurus** [BAY-pyow-sore-us] was the **record holder** for the largest feathered dinosaur. It was **40 times lighter** than Yutyrannus!

2
1
3

83

FEARSOME FISH-EATERS

Dinosaur **fossil finds** reveal that not all dinosaurs ate meat. Some fancied **fish** for tea!

Suchomimus had over 100 teeth but they weren't very sharp. Its **long snout**, about 2 m in length, was perfect for catching fish.

This toothy beast is a **Suchomimus**, pronounced **sook-oh-mim-us**. Its name means crocodile mimic.

Suchomimus was a dinosaur that may have dined on **fish** as well as meat. It roamed the river banks of **Early Cretaceous period Africa** looking for prey.

Scientists wonder if Suchomimus may have **swum** and **dived** for food too.

Suchomimus was huge! It was 11 m long and 3 m tall. It weighed 2,700 kg.

Suchomimus would have needed **large prey** to satisfy its appetite. It probably feasted on **Mawsonia** [maw-SO-nee-ah], a big **prehistoric fish** that could grow up to 4 m long. That's about the same size as a rhinoceros!

Baryonyx's **claw** on its thumb was **30 cm long** - that's a bit longer than the height of your average dinosaur book! It may have used the large claw to **spear fish**.

Baryonyx was a fish-eating dinosaur that lived during the Early Cretaceous period. Its **crocodile-like jaws** were perfect for snatching fish from the water.

This scary creature is a **Baryonyx**, pronounced **bah-ree-ON-icks**. Its name means heavy claw.

Fish-eating dinosaurs used their **long jaws** and **strong necks** to grab their prey out of the water with powerful, darting strikes.

Palaeontologists know that Baryonyx was a **fish-eater** because **fish scales** have been found in the stomach region of some **fossil** discoveries.

Baryonyx's **jagged teeth** curved inwards to make it hard for a fish to escape!

85

BURIED BONES

Palaeontologists use fossil finds to learn about mighty meat-eating dinosaurs of the past. The fossil pieces fit together like a jigsaw puzzle to reveal what the dinosaur looked like and how it lived.

Tyrannosaurus rex had around 200 bones in its body.

T. rex fought one another.
One famous T. rex fossil, Sue, had **bite** marks on her face from another T. rex!

Fossilised dinosaur poo, called **coprolite**, was found in Canada. It probably came from a T. rex and was the size of a sandwich. The coprolite contained bones from another dinosaur – maybe a young Triceratops.

In 1971, the fossil of a **Velociraptor** and **Protoceratops** [pro-toe-ker-ah-tops] locked in a **fierce** battle was found in the Gobi Desert, Mongolia. The Velociraptor was grasping its **prey** with its forelimbs and claws, while the Protoceratops tried to defend itself by biting the arm of its attacker!

A bone from a **pterosaur** was discovered in the fossilised remains of a **Velociraptor**. Pterosaurs had wingspans of 2 m or more. That's only a little bigger than the length of its attacker! It would have been difficult and dangerous to hunt a pterosaur, so this bone was probably from a carcass.

The red dots show dinosaur **fossil** 'hotspots'. They are places where large numbers of fossils have been discovered, such as in parts of South America and China.

In the 4th century, a Chinese historian called **Chang Qu** mislabelled a dinosaur fossil as a **dragon bone**! Oops!

QUICK KILLER FACTS

Meat-eating dinosaurs were some of the fiercest creatures to ever walk the Earth. Check out these fun dino facts!

ALLOSAURUS

HEIGHT: 3 m

LENGTH: 12 m

WEIGHT: 2,100 kg

LIVED: Late Jurassic

LOCATION: Portugal, USA

FIRST FOSSIL DISCOVERY: Colorado, USA, 1869

FACT: Allosaurus poo has been found measuring 1.5 m – about the size of a car!

COELOPHYSIS

HEIGHT: 1.8 m

LENGTH: 3 m

WEIGHT: 27 kg

LIVED: Late Jurassic

LOCATION: USA

FIRST FOSSIL DISCOVERY: New Mexico, USA, 1881

FACT: It is thought that Coelophysis bit their prey like Komodo dragons do today.

UTAHRAPTOR

HEIGHT: 1.7 m

LENGTH: 6 m

WEIGHT: 1,000 kg

LIVED: Early Cretaceous

LOCATION: USA

FIRST FOSSIL DISCOVERY: Utah, USA, 1975

FACT: Utahraptor is the largest raptor discovered to date.

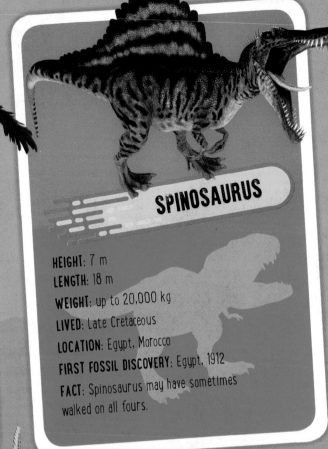

SPINOSAURUS

HEIGHT: 7 m

LENGTH: 18 m

WEIGHT: up to 20,000 kg

LIVED: Late Cretaceous

LOCATION: Egypt, Morocco

FIRST FOSSIL DISCOVERY: Egypt, 1912

FACT: Spinosaurus may have sometimes walked on all fours.

MICRORAPTOR

HEIGHT: 0.3 m

LENGTH: 0.8 m

WEIGHT: 1-2 kg

LIVED: Early Cretaceous

LOCATION: China

FIRST FOSSIL DISCOVERY: Liaoning, China, 2000

FACT: This meat-eater ate birds, so it might have spent some of its life high up in trees.

DEINONYCHUS

HEIGHT: 0.9 m

LENGTH: 3 m

WEIGHT: 75 kg

LIVED: Early Cretaceous

LOCATION: USA

FIRST FOSSIL DISCOVERY: Montana, USA, 1931

FACT: Deinonychus had the same bite force as an alligator.

DINOSAUR
BABIES

EGGS OF ALL KINDS

Just like dinosaurs themselves, **dinosaur eggs** varied in **size**, **shape** and **texture**.

Dinosaurs are related to modern **birds** and, like birds, they laid **eggs**.

Hypacrosaurus

Some dinosaur eggs were **round** and as big as a football, and others were **oval-shaped** like a raindrop. They had **hard shells** that were roughly the same thickness as a turtle eggshell, about 45 mm.

Eggs were usually laid in **clutches**, sometimes up to **30** or **40 eggs** in **one nest**.

The first dinosaur **egg fragments** ever found were **discovered** by a priest called Jean-Jacques Pouech in the **Pyrenees mountains** in France, in 1859. At first, Pouech thought the pieces of shell belonged to an enormous bird egg or were pieces of armadillo shell!

Some **eggs** were **enormous!** The egg of the duck-billed dinosaur **Hypacrosaurus** [hi-PAK-roh-sore-us] weighed **4 kg**. That's as much as an adult cat.

Protoceratops

Once **hatched**, dinosaur babies **grew** big and they grew **fast** – five times faster than a human baby! Dinosaurs might have become **extinct**, in part, because their **eggs** took so **long** to **hatch**.

Scientists think **dinosaur embryos** incubated for different lengths of time. As with birds, it all depended on the **size** of the dinosaur species. A **Protoceratops** embryo **hatched** from golf ball-sized eggs after **three months**. The babies of bigger dinosaurs, like **Hypacrosaurus**, didn't emerge until **six months** after the eggs had been laid. By comparison, small **modern bird** eggs can be ready to hatch in about **11 days** or for larger birds about **80 days**.

JUVENILE DINOSAURS

Once they **hatched**, baby dinosaurs **grew quickly**.
Like humans, dinosaurs grew from **babies** into
juveniles before becoming **adults**.

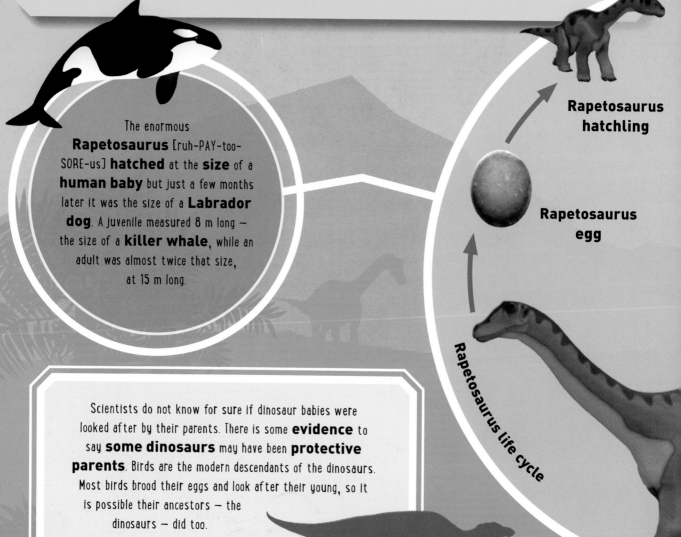

The enormous
Rapetosaurus [ruh-PAY-too-
SORE-us] **hatched** at the **size** of a
human baby but just a few months
later it was the size of a **Labrador
dog**. A juvenile measured 8 m long —
the size of a **killer whale**, while an
adult was almost twice that size,
at 15 m long.

Rapetosaurus
hatchling

Rapetosaurus
egg

Rapetosaurus life cycle

Scientists do not know for sure if dinosaur babies were
looked after by their parents. There is some **evidence** to
say **some dinosaurs** may have been **protective
parents**. Birds are the modern descendants of the dinosaurs.
Most birds brood their eggs and look after their young, so it
is possible their ancestors — the
dinosaurs — did too.

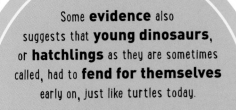

Some **evidence** also suggests that **young dinosaurs,** or **hatchlings** as they are sometimes called, had to **fend for themselves** early on, just like turtles today.

As dinosaurs grew up into **juveniles,** they may have **grouped together** in **herds** for **protection** and to find **food.** A herd of about 25 juvenile **Sinornithomimus dongi** [sine-or-nith-oh-MEEM-us dong-ee] fell into a **mud trap** on the edge of a lake in Mongolia. Their bones were preserved for 90 million years.

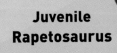

Juvenile Rapetosaurus

Adult Rapetosaurus

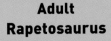

Dinosaurs **reproduced** when they were still **young** themselves. Fossil finds of dinosaurs that were just **eight years old** showed they had already **laid eggs.**

The discovery of **eggs** near a female **Tyrannosaurus rex** [tie-RAN-oh-sore-us rex] fossil revealed that this dinosaur was **still developing** when it became a **mother** at **18 years old.** A T. rex wasn't **fully grown** until it was about **20 years old** and lived for up to 28 years.

95

TYRANNOSAURUS REX BABIES

We know **Tyrannosaurus rex** was one of the **fiercest** dinosaurs to ever walk the Earth. The **Cretaceous** meat-eater had **60 sharp teeth** in its powerful jaws, a nasty bite and could grow up to **12 m long**. But, no nests or eggs of T. rex have ever been found.

T. rex probably **laid** its eggs in a **similar way** to other **theropods** (meat-eating dinosaurs) – at least two eggs at a time and up to **16 eggs** in a **circle** inside its **nest**.

Each **egg** would have been **large** too – about the size of a large loaf of bread.

The **nest** was probably an **enormous 3 m wide**. That's about the same length as two bikes end to end!

We know T. rex is thought to have had **feathers**. Perhaps its **young** were born with a **fluffy feather coat** to keep them **warm** too!

The **discovery** of a **juvenile** T. rex is **rare**. Experts think this dinosaur's ability to find food and thrive meant most young T. rex individuals **survived** into **adulthood**.

In 1942, the **skull** of a very **young T. rex** was found in Montana in the USA. It **looked very different** to the skull of an adult T. rex. Its **snout** was very **narrow** while an adult skull was more robust. It also had **more teeth**, suggesting the dinosaur might have lost teeth as it grew into an adult.

T. rex hatched as a small baby and quickly grew into a one-tonne juvenile. Then, between the **ages of 14 and 18** it had a **growth spurt**. It piled on about **1,700 kg a year**. That's about half the weight of a car in a year! In about four years, a T. rex went from one tonne to six tonnes!

STEGOSAURUS BABIES

We know **Stegosaurus** lived in the **Late Jurassic period** (155 to 145 mya). It was an **enormous**, slow-moving **plant-eater** that grew to about **9 m long** – the length of a bus. But, we know very little about the eggs and nests of this plant-eating dinosaur, as no eggs or nests have been found yet.

It's thought that Stegosaurus might have **laid** between **20** and **30 eggs**.

Lots of **eggs** would probably have been **eaten** by **predators**, such as **raptors**, before they hatched.

To **grow** to the enormous **size** and **weight** of an adult Stegosaurus, a baby had to grow quickly. It might have put on as much as **14 kg a day**. That's the same growth rate as some whales.

The Stegosaurus baby or **hatchling** was probably only a few hours old when it died. The hatchling was **no bigger than a cat** - about one-eleventh of an adult stegosaurus' 9-m length and 3-m height.

In 2007, the **fossilised footprints** of a **baby** Stegosaurus were found in Colorado, USA. Each print was only about the **size** of a **large coin.**

The baby's **footprint** was found alongside the footprints of **adults** and **bigger juveniles**. This suggests Stegosaurus may have **lived** and **travelled** in **groups.**

TRICERATOPS BABIES

We know Triceratops was a **three-horned,** **plant-eating** dinosaur that lived during the **Late Cretaceous** period (68 to 66 mya). They could be **9 m long** and weigh as much as **5,500 kg.** That's as heavy as two elephants! But, not much is known about the size of a Triceratops' egg or its nest.

Fossils of **Triceratops babies, juveniles** and **adults** help us learn about Triceratops.

Even if Triceratops did not stay with its **eggs,** it's possible it may have **guarded** its nest from **predators,** such as prehistoric crocodiles.

Triceratops probably **laid** its **eggs** in a **nest,** but it may not have **brooded** the eggs in case it squashed them with its heavy weight!

A Triceratops **hatchling** was possibly only **12 cm long** – about the size of a melon.

In 1997, the **skull** of a **baby Triceratops** was found in Montana, USA. It belonged to a **one-year-old dinosaur infant** that was the same size as a sheep.

The **30-cm skull** had **short horns, huge eyes** and a **short face,** which were all common features of adult Triceratops.

A **juvenile's horns** were **stubby** and **pointed backwards**. As it grew, its horns straightened out and turned to face forwards, ready to **defend** their owner from **attack**.

The **baby's horns** suggest that Triceratops didn't just have horns to **attract** a mate. One idea is that the **frill** and horns **helped** juvenile Triceratops **recognise** each other.

TROODON BABIES

It is believed that **Troodon** was one of the **cleverest dinosaurs** because it had a very **large brain** compared to its small body. It was a meat-eating dinosaur that lived during the **Cretaceous** period. Several Troodon nests have been found.

Troodon **laid** its **eggs upright** in mud, so the tops remained in the air. This is different from other reptiles, such as crocodiles, which bury their eggs. The eggs were **shaped** like **raindrops** and laid so that they all pointed toward the middle of the nest.

Egg clutches found in Alberta, Canada and Montana, USA, suggest a Troodon **nest** was a **1-m circle** with an obvious edge.

A **female Troodon** produced about **two eggs a day** over a **week** or **two**. It laid up to **24 eggs** in a nest. It took about two weeks to lay a large clutch of eggs.

The dinosaur probably **kept** the **eggs warm** with its body, and **males** may have **brooded** the eggs as well as females.

When the **baby** Troodon dinosaurs **hatched**, they were **fully formed**. The hatchlings quickly learned how to **hunt** for food and **defend** themselves from large predators.

An area of **Montana** in the USA has been nicknamed '**Egg Mountain**'. This is because the remains of lots of dinosaurs and their nests have been found there, including Troodon nests.

One Troodon **nest** on Egg Mountain contained **eggs**, **baby** Troodon dinosaur skeletons, the skeleton of an **adult** Troodon and the bones of a small plant-eating dinosaur called **Orodromeus** [or-oh-DROM-ee-us]. One theory is the adult Troodon had killed Orodromeus and was bringing it back to **feed** its young.

Orodromeus

PROTOCERATOPS BABIES

Protoceratops belonged to the same family of dinosaurs as Triceratops but it was a lot smaller, about the **size** of a **big pig**. Its size meant it was often the **prey** of bigger, fiercer meat-eaters.

Each Protoceratops **egg** was about **20 cm long**. That's about as long as a large banana.

Protoceratops' **eggs** were **laid** in **spirals**, with up to **18 eggs** in each **nest**.

In 1994, **two small bowl-shaped nests** were discovered in the Gobi Desert in Asia, each with **15 baby Protoceratops** skeletons inside. The infants' heads were all facing the same direction, away from the windy desert. Were they trying to protect themselves from the weather?

Protoceratops **eggs incubated** for about **80 days** before hatching.

In 2011, another **nest** was found in **Mongolia** that contained the remains of about **15 babies**, each no more than a year old. The dinosaur babies were between **10 and 15 cm long**. It's possible these babies were being cared for by their parents after they had hatched. They may have been **buried** alive by a **snowstorm**.

A **young** Protoceratops had a very **large head** compared to the rest of its body. This is true of many animals, including human babies!

DIPLODOCUS BABIES

We know **Diplodocus** was a **slow-moving sauropod** from the Late Jurassic period. It walked on **four legs** and had a **long neck** and a very **long tail** that it would use like a **whip**, to fend off **attackers**. We also know their nests had something in common with modern turtles – they were underground.

Despite its huge size, Diplodocus' **eggs** were actually quite **small**. Each one was about the size of an **ostrich egg** (15 cm tall and 13 cm wide), even though an adult Diplodocus was much heavier than a fully grown ostrich.

The **eggs** were **laid** in **underground nests**, the same as sea turtle nests, where they **hatched** after about **42 days**. A big dinosaur like Diplodocus probably couldn't sit on its eggs. It might have flattened them!

As many as **30 eggs** could be **laid** in the nest and possibly **covered** with **plants** to keep them **safe** and **warm**.

Diplodocus may have laid more **clutches of eggs** at **different nesting sites**. If one egg clutch was eaten by other creatures such as snakes or lizards, another would still have been **safely hidden**.

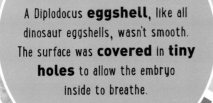

A Diplodocus **eggshell**, like all dinosaur eggshells, wasn't smooth. The surface was **covered** in **tiny holes** to allow the embryo inside to breathe.

One **predator** of sauropod eggs was a snake called **Sanajeh indicus** [san-AH-jay IN-deh-cuss]. Sauropod eggs found in 1987 were discovered with the bones of this ancient predator coiled around them. This **3.5-m snake** was waiting for a hatchling when it was probably buried by a landslide.

Diplodocus' **short incubation** time meant **more eggs** had a **chance** to **hatch** before being discovered and eaten by predators.

As they grew up, **juvenile** Diplodocus may have **grouped** together in **herds** for protection.

Hatchlings had to **grow quickly**. In about ten years, a Diplodocus baby grew from **30 cm** to **26 m long** – the length of three buses.

OVIRAPTOR BABIES

Oviraptor was a dinosaur that lived during the **Late Cretaceous** period. It ate fruit, eggs, shellfish and meat. It was a fierce hunter, with strong back legs, short arms and sharp claws. It brooded and protected its eggs in its nest.

Oviraptor could **lay** up to **20 eggs** at a time. They were placed in a **circular pattern** and **stacked** in two or three **layers**.

Its **eggs** were probably **blue-green**. In living birds, such as emus, blue-green eggs are often **looked after** by the **male parent**. The same might have been true of Oviraptor.

Oviraptor **eggs** were **18 cm long** and **6.5 cm wide**. They were shaped a bit like a **potato**.

Oviraptors **brooded** their eggs to about **35-40 °C** - the same as chickens. After **45 days' incubation**, the babies were ready to **hatch**.

Oviraptor was first **discovered** in the Gobi Desert in 1923. Its name means '**egg thief**'. It got its name because the first fossil was found amongst a **nest** of what scientists thought were Protoceratops eggs at the time. They later turned out to be Oviraptor eggs. The adult fossil was probably a **parent guarding** or **brooding** its nest.

In 1993, another Oviraptor fossil was **found** with a nest of similar-looking eggs. The **embryos** inside were Oviraptor babies, not Protoceratops. The Oviraptor was **lying across its eggs** with its arms spread wide, **protecting** its **eggs**, not stealing them. The dinosaur might have died protecting the nest from a **sandstorm** or **flood**.

If Oviraptor cared for its eggs, its **feathered arms** might have **protected** the **eggs** from the sun during the day and kept them warm at night.

MAIASAURA BABIES

Maiasaura, 'good mother lizard', belonged to a group of dinosaurs called hadrosaurs. Like other hadrosaurs, we know Maiasaura lived in herds and may have even nested in colonies.

Between 1977 and 1979, scientists discovered 14 nests at 'Egg Mountain' in Montana. This was the nesting site of individual Maiasaura. Hundreds of fossils of eggs, juveniles and adult Maiasaura have now been found at the site.

Each egg was about the size of a grapefruit.

Some scientists think Maiasaura didn't sit on the eggs to keep them warm but used rotting plants to heat the nest – stinky!

The nests were small hollows in the mud and each one was wider than the length of a lion – at about 2 m wide. They contained 30 to 40 eggs in each and the nests were about 6 m apart. This suggests Maiasaura grouped together during breeding season.

Maiasaura was as big as a school bus and weighed 4,400 kg. A **hatchling** was about **30 cm** and weighed just **1 kg**. That's about the same size as a meerkat.

It's possible that Maiasaura **babies** were **helpless** when they **hatched** and were **looked after** by their **parents**.

A **hatchling** started life with a **large head** and **short tail**. As it grew, the dinosaur's body and tail would have caught up with its head!

The presence of **hatchlings, juveniles, eggs** and **embryos** in one site, suggest these dinosaurs stuck **together**. In fact, **fossils** revealed that the babies found in nests had **worn teeth** from eating food, so the **parents** probably **brought food** to the hatchlings.

However, some scientists do not think Maiasaura stayed with her hatchlings. These experts suggest the **parents** were **not** **around** after the baby dinosaurs **hatched**. Instead, like **baby iguanas**, they think the Maiasaura hatchlings stayed in a **group**. A Maiasaura predator could only eat one baby dinosaur at a time, so it was **safer** to stay together.

Perhaps the **hatchlings** fed on the **rotten plants** in the nest rather than food brought to them by their parents!

VELOCIRAPTOR BABIES

Velociraptor was a **fierce hunter**. This feathered meat-eater hunted during the **Late Cretaceous** period, but scientists have not found fossil eggs or nests of Velociraptor.

The **fossils** of other raptors, such as **Oviraptor**, and what we know about modern birds, offer **clues** about Velociraptor.

Velociraptor looked a bit like a funny **bird of prey.** Some experts suggest it may have behaved in a similar way to eagles, too. A male and a female might have **paired up** during the **breeding** season and made a **nest** together.

Like Oviraptor, Velociraptor possibly **brooded** its eggs, using its **feathers** to keep the eggs cool during hot, sunny days, and warm during cold, windy weather.

Two fossils of infant Velociraptor **skulls** reveal they had **shorter snouts** and **bigger eyes** than adults.

Velociraptor was about the **size** of a **turkey** but its **eggs** were probably a bit bigger than a chicken egg and shaped like a **teardrop**.

One **nest** in the Gobi Desert showed something very curious – **two tiny skulls** of Velociraptors were found near the nest of an **Oviraptor**. How did they get there? Perhaps the babies were trying to steal the Oviraptor eggs or maybe the baby Velociraptors were **lunch** for the adult Oviraptor!

One exciting **theory** is that a female **Velociraptor** placed the eggs near **Oviraptor's** nest to hand the **parenting** to another species, much like **cuckoos** do today. Maybe the babies had hatched and were running away …

ICHTHYOSAUR BABIES

Ichthyosaurs were **marine reptiles** that lived during the **Mesozoic era**, at the same time as the dinosaurs. Like modern dolphins, ichthyosaurs were **strong swimmers** that had large eyes to spot their prey in the water.

Ichthyosaurs gave birth to **live young** - one or two **pups**. Each pup was **fully developed** when it was born and it could swim, hunt fish and fend for itself straight away.

The young were **born tail first**. This is so they didn't **drown** as they were being born. Ichthyosaurs never came up on to land but they did need to **breathe** air.

Although most females gave birth to one or two pups, one **fossilised pregnant ichthyosaur** shows **11 babies** inside the mother! Scientists think this was **unusual**.

Experts have discovered that some ichthyosaurs gave **birth** to **young** with **teeth** while the **adults** had **toothless snouts**. This suggests the babies' **diet** may have been different to the parents'.

In 2017, a pregnant ichthyosaur was found with an incomplete baby still growing inside. The **embryo** was only **7 cm long**, and had ribs, a fore fin and the bones of its spine were visible. Its **mother** was **3.5 m long** – that's about the same size as a small hammerhead shark!

Baby ichthyosaurs could probably **swim quickly** after fish in shallow water. As they grew, the young **joined** their **parents** in **deeper water**, where they **hunted** jellyfish and squid.

Nearly 200 mya, a young Ichthyosaur **ate** a **squid** and then died with its meal still **undigested** in its **stomach**! The baby was just under **half a metre long**, while its **parents** could reach **4.5 m** – a bit bigger than a bottlenose dolphin. This baby ichthyosaur had a lot of growing to do, so it had a lot of eating to do!

QUICK EGG-CELLENT FACTS

Experts are discovering more and more information about dinosaur nests, eggs and babies. Check out these fascinating dinosaur egg facts!

Trillions of dinosaur eggs were laid throughout the Mesozoic era and there were more than 1,500 species of dinosaur. So far, about 40 different kinds of dinosaur eggs have been found.

Mussaurus laid some of the smallest dinosaur eggs – they were only about 2.5 cm.

Eggs and the fossil bones of young dinosaurs have been found on every continent except Antarctica.

Dinosaur babies were eaten by other prehistoric animals. A fossil of Repenomamus robustus [re-pe-no-MAY-mus rob-US-tuss] found in the year 2000 had the remains of a baby Psittacosaurus [SIT-ak-oh-sore-us] inside.

Dinosaur babies could sometimes do what their parents couldn't! Fossilised footprints the size of tennis balls reveal that a baby Apatosaurus could stand on its back legs. Its enormous parents could not have done that!

FIRST WHOLE EGG

WHEN: 1930
WHERE: France
FOUND BY: Jean-Jacques Pouech
FACT: When the egg was ploughed up in a field nobody knew what it was. They thought it belonged to a giant bird.

LARGEST EGGS

WHEN: Early 1990s
WHERE: China
FOUND BY: A farmer
FACT: The largest eggs found to date are 0.5 m in length and laid by a giant oviraptorosauria. One embryo inside was nicknamed Baby Louie.

SPACE BABY

WHEN: 1985
DINOSAUR: Maiasaura bone and bits of eggshell
ROCKET: Spacelab 2
ASTRONAUT: Loren Acton
FACT: A piece of Maiasaura eggshell was sent into space.

FURRY BABY

WHEN: 2010
WHERE: Germany
WHAT: The fossil of a Sciurumimus [SIGH-oor-uh-MEEM-us] hatchling about 70 cm long.
FACT: A baby Sciurumimus had a layer of soft feather-like fur on its tail – a bit like a squirrel. This is why its name means squirrel mimic.

SEA AND SKY
MONSTERS

PREHISTORIC NEIGHBOURS

During the **Mesozoic era**, dinosaurs shared their world with the sea monsters **ichthyosaurs** as well as **plesiosaurs** [PLEE-see-oh-sores] and **pterosaurs** [TER-oh-sores], which soared high in the skies.

Giant reptiles soared high in the sky and **marine monsters** swam in the seas and oceans, too.

This flying creature is **Dimorphodon**, pronounced DIE-more-foh-don. Its name means two-formed tooth, because it had two kinds of teeth.

Plesiosaurs were **meat-eating marine reptiles**. They used their **flippers** to move through the water.

Most plesiosaurs had **long necks** to help them **strike out** and **catch their prey**.

Flying reptiles called **pterosaurs** first appeared at the end of the **Triassic period** (248–206 mya). Triassic pterosaurs like Dimorphodon were **small** compared to their Cretaceous cousins that lived 144–65 mya.

A **pterosaur's tail** may have helped it **change direction** during flight.

Some pterosaurs were as big as small aeroplanes. Others were as small as sparrows.

Pterosaurs had **wings** that stretched from their legs to their arm bones and across a long **'flight' finger**.

Pliosaurs [PLY-oh-sore] were **a type of short-necked plesiosaur.** They had **huge heads** and very sharp **crocodile-like teeth**!

Pliosaurs were **so big** that **Tyrannosaurus rex** would have been **a snack** for these enormous beasts!

MONSTERS OF THE SEA

Dinosaurs may have ruled the land, but the **prehistoric monsters of the sea** were not dinosaurs. They were **fierce aquatic reptiles** that lurked in the watery depths below.

FOOD → CHAIN

Liopleurodon, pronounced LIE-oh-PLOOR-oh-don, means smooth-sided teeth.

Liopleurodon was an **enormous pliosaur** with huge teeth. At **45 cm**, each **tooth** was twice the size of a Tyrannosaurus rex's.

Liopleurodon may have grown to 25 m. That's as long as a blue whale!

Prehistoric sea creatures were part of a **food chain**, just like the dinosaurs on land. **Squid** would have been **eaten by reptiles** like ichthyosaurs. They, in turn, would have been a **tasty lunch for larger reptiles** such as Liopleurodon.

Ichthyosaurs were **giant reptiles** that lived during the Jurassic period (206-144 mya). They are often called '**sea dragons**'.

At **21 m long**, Shastasaurus [shass-tah-SORE-us] is the **biggest known ichthyosaur**. It didn't have any teeth but may have sucked its prey into its mouth.

ichthyosaur

Ichthyosaurs had **large eyes**. Temnodontosaurus [tem-NO-don-tuh-SORE-us] had eyes **as big as dinner plates**. It probably dived into the dark sea depths looking for food.

squid

Ichthyosaurs used their **speed** to quickly dart away from **predators**, such as Liopleurodon.

It's been said that the **Loch Ness Monster** is a **plesiosaur** that got **trapped in the loch** when the sea retreated millions of years ago.

INCREDIBLE
ICHTHYOSAURUS

The most famous ichthyosaur is **Ichthyosaurus**. It may have looked like a **dolphin** but this **prehistoric reptile** was, in fact, a distant relative of lizards and snakes. It lived during the **Late Triassic** (237–206 mya) and **Early Jurassic periods** (206–174 mya).

Ichthyosaurus, pronounced ICK-thee-oh-SORE-us. means fish lizard.

Ichthyosaurus had **four fins** on the sides of its body and a dorsal (back) fin to keep it stable in the water. It moved its **fish-like tail fin** from side to side to **propel** itself through the water.

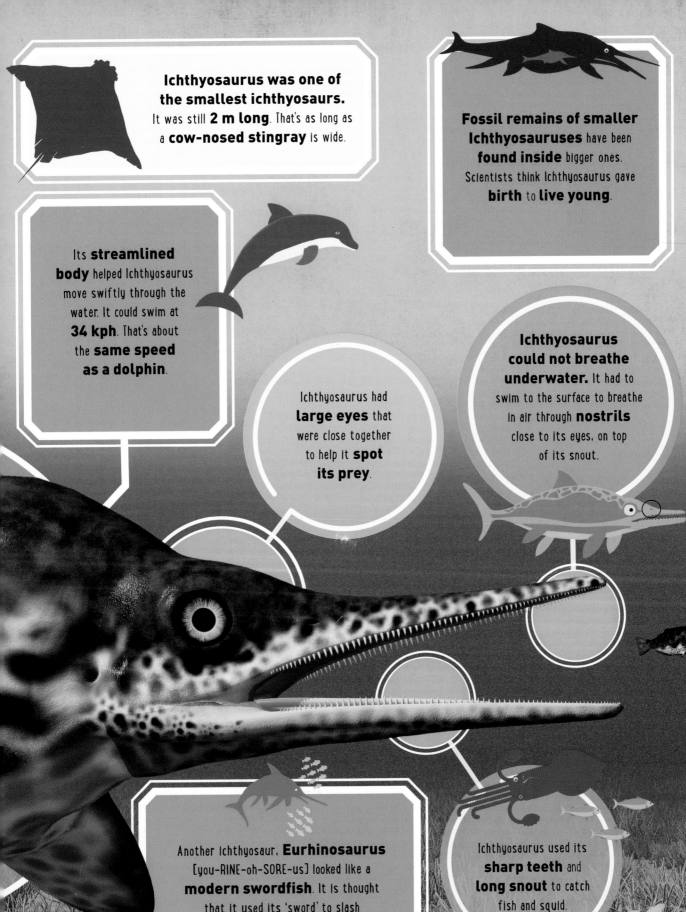

Ichthyosaurus was one of the smallest ichthyosaurs. It was still **2 m long**. That's as long as a **cow-nosed stingray** is wide.

Fossil remains of smaller Ichthyosauruses have been **found inside** bigger ones. Scientists think Ichthyosaurus gave **birth** to **live young**.

Its **streamlined body** helped Ichthyosaurus move swiftly through the water. It could swim at **34 kph**. That's about the **same speed as a dolphin**.

Ichthyosaurus had **large eyes** that were close together to help it **spot its prey**.

Ichthyosaurus could not breathe underwater. It had to swim to the surface to breathe in air through **nostrils** close to its eyes, on top of its snout.

Another ichthyosaur, **Eurhinosaurus** [you-RINE-oh-SORE-us] looked like a **modern swordfish**. It is thought that it used its 'sword' to slash through shoals of small fish.

Ichthyosaurus used its **sharp teeth** and **long snout** to catch fish and squid.

POWERFUL PLESIOSAURS AND PLIOSAURS

Plesiosaurs first appeared in the **Late Triassic era** and lived through the rest of the **Mesozoic era**. These **enormous meat-eaters** feasted on huge amounts of fish, squid and molluscs!

Elasmosaurus was **14 m long**. Its **neck** was **7 m** - half its full length. A giraffe's neck is only 1.8 m!

This plesiosaur is an **Elasmosaurus**, pronounced el-AZ-moh-sore-us. Its name means thin-plated lizard.

Some **plesiosaurs swallowed stones** that acted as **weights to help them sink** to the ocean floor in search of food.

Plesiosaurs had big front **flippers** and smaller back flippers. They used them to **swim in the same way turtles do today**.

Plesiosaurs had **long, pointed teeth** for capturing rather than chewing their prey. They probably **swallowed their food whole!**

These marine reptiles lived in the oceans but they couldn't breathe underwater. They **needed to go to the surface for air.**

Plesiosaurs had long necks, small heads and wide bodies.

Liopleurodon, a pliosaur (see p 6), was a huge **aquatic predator** but it didn't have speed on its side. It **swam at about 10 kph**. That's about the **same as an otter**. Its jaws were longer than a canoe.

Pliosaurs were a type of plesiosaur. They had **large heads** with **strong jaws** and **short necks**.

This pliosaur is a **Kronosaurus**, pronounced CROW-noh-SORE-us.

Pliosaurs had bigger back flippers than front ones.

At **11 m long**, Kronosaurus was **bigger than an orca**!

Pliosaurs ate plesiosaurs!
A fossil of Elasmosaurus was found with bite marks from the giant pliosaur Kronosaurus.

By the end of the **Cretaceous period**, plesiosaurs and pliosaurs had to **make way** for the mighty **mosasaurs**.

MIGHTY MOSASAURS

The mosasaurs [MO-zah-sore] were the rulers of the waves during the **Late Cretaceous period**. Fossils have been found on almost every continent of the world, so mosasaurs were as widespread in the water as the dinosaurs were on land!

This mosasaur is a **Tylosaurus**, pronounced TIE-loh-sore-us. Its name means knob lizard.

Mosasaurs moved the back of their body and their **long tail** from side to side to **propel** themselves through the water.

Hainosaurus [HIGH-no-SORE-us] was a mosasaur that grew to about **12 m long** – about the **length of a humpback whale**.

Mosasaurs could expand their jaws to eat their prey whole, like a snake.

Most mosasaurs had **fish, plesiosaurs, turtles, ammonites** and other **mosasaurs** for their **lunch**.

Mosasaurs had **one enemy** – prehistoric **sharks**! One fossil has the marks of a shark's teeth in its spine.

Tylosaurus used its **snout** when **attacking prey** rather than its teeth. It would **ram** it with such force that its prey would be stunned.

Globidens
[GLO-bih-denz] was a mosasaur with **rounded teeth**. It used its teeth to **crush prey** such as **turtles and shellfish**.

A **Hainosaurus fossil** has been found with part of a **giant turtle** in its stomach!

Mosasaurs became **extinct** at the **same time as the last of the dinosaurs**, around **65 mya**.

MEGA MEGALODON

Megalodon was an enormous **prehistoric shark** that is possibly the most **fearsome predator** to have ever lived. It roamed the seas between 23 and 2.6 mya, after the age of the dinosaurs.

The height of Megalodon's **tail fin** alone was **4 m**. That's about the **same length as a male great white shark**.

Megalodon, pronounced MEG-ah-low-don, means big tooth.

Megalodons lived in all oceans of the world. They **hunted** in the **open sea** and may have **rushed from below**, taking their prey by surprise.

This mighty creature **weighed** about 60,000 kg. That's more than **70 giant squids!**

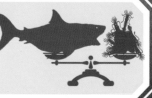

Megalodon ate **giant turtles**, **whales** and **mammals** such as Odobenocetops [oh-doh-ben-OH-set-ops].

Megalodon possibly **tore off the fins of large prey** first so it couldn't swim away.

In **one bite** of its **gigantic jaws**, Megalodon could have **crushed a car** with a force up to **30 times stronger than that of a lion**.

Its jaws were home to 276 giant teeth in six rows.

Megalodon's **fossilised teeth** were once **mistaken for dragon tongues**. Each one was **17 cm long** – about the length of a banana.

Megalodon was about **18 m long**. That's as long as **three great white sharks**.

THE BIG, THE BAD AND THE UGLY

Prehistoric seas were full of weird and wonderful creatures, just like the oceans today. Here are some of the prehistoric creatures that once lived beneath the waves ...

ARCHELON

PRONUNCIATION: ARK-eh-lon

TYPE: Reptile

SIZE: 4.6 m

LIVED: Late Cretaceous

PREDATORS: Mosasaurs and sharks

FACT: This turtle was twice as big as the largest turtle today – the leatherback.

CRASSIGYRINUS

PRONUNCIATION: CRASS-ee-jih-RYE-nuss

TYPE: Early amphibian

SIZE: Up to 2 m long

LIVED: 359–323 mya

PREDATORS: Unknown

FACT: Crassigyrinus had unusually large jaws, which had two rows of sharp teeth, including a pair of fangs in the second row. It probably swallowed its prey whole.

DUNKLEOSTEUS

PRONUNCIATION: dunk-lee-OWE-stee-us

TYPE: Fish

SIZE: 8-10 m long

LIVED: 370-360 mya

PREDATORS: None

FACT: For such a fierce predator, it didn't have any teeth. Dunkleosteus used bony plates with sharp points to bite through its prey.

STETHACANTHUS

PRONUNCIATION: STETH-ac-anth-us

TYPE: Fish

SIZE: 0.7-2 m long

LIVED: 370-345 mya

PREDATORS: Dunkleosteus

FACT: Surfs up! Stethacanthus was a shark with a dorsal fin shaped like a surfboard. It would have had no problem recognising others of its own species.

LEEDSICHTHYS

PRONUNCIATION: Leeds-ICK-thees

TYPE: Fish

SIZE: Up to 27 m long

LIVED: Late Jurassic

PREDATORS: Liopleurodon

FACT: Possibly the largest fish ever to have lived. It had 40,000 teeth that filtered the water to pick out tiny shrimp, jellyfish and small fish.

PTERYGOTUS

PRONUNCIATION: terry-GO-tuss

TYPE: Giant sea scorpion

SIZE: Up to 2.3 m long

LIVED: 444-389 mya

PREDATORS: Armoured fish such as Dunkleosteus

FACT: Fossils of Pterygotus have been found on every continent except Antarctica.

EARLY MONSTERS OF THE SKIES

Dinosaurs probably didn't fly but the skies weren't empty during the **Mesozoic era**. **Flying reptiles**, called **pterosaurs**, flew above the Earth. They first appeared during the **Triassic period**.

This flying creature is an **Austriadactylus** pronounced OSS-tree-ah-dak-tyl-us. Its name means Austria finger.

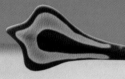
Triassic pterosaurs were the **first animals to fly**, apart from insects. Their **wings** were made of **skin**, **muscles** and other **body tissues**.

Early pterosaurs were small, with long, narrow tails and wings.

Most pterosaurs lived near water and ate fish and shellfish. Some species lived further inland. They probably **ate young dinosaurs, eggs, insects and other animals**.

When **on land**, pterosaurs **walked on all fours** like vampire bats. They used all four limbs to launch themselves into the air.

Pterosaurs had **hollow bones**. This meant they could get **up into the air** easily – although **bigger pterosaurs** needed a bit of **a run up**!

Some pterosaurs could **fly** at **speeds of 120 kph** - that's **as fast as a running cheetah!**

Many pterosaurs sported **head crests**. The crests may have been used to **attract a mate** or to **get rid of heat as they flew**.

Young pterosaurs could probably survive on their own as soon as they hatched. Their wings helped them get into the air and away from predators as quickly as possible.

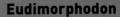
pterosaur wing

Their **large wings** were supported in the air by an **extra long fourth finger**.

Eudimorphodon [you-DIE-mor-fo-don] was an early pterosaur from the Triassic period. It had **100 teeth** in its long jaws!

Later Cretaceous pterosaurs grew to enormous sizes. Some may have lived in large **flocks**, hunting on foot **like herons**.

Pterosaurs disappeared from Earth along with the dinosaurs 65 mya.

IMPRESSIVE PTERANODON

Pteranodon was a flying reptile that existed during the **Late Cretaceous period**, about 75 mya. This massive creature lived near the **coast of North America** and probably had a **diet of fish and squid**.

Pteranodon, pronounced teh-RAN-oh-don, means no teeth.

Like many Cretaceous pterosaurs, Pteranodon had a **short tail**, **big wings** and a **large head**.

Pteranodon spent most of its days **flying** over the **sea** and hardly any time on land.

Its **wing shape** meant it could **fly much like an eagle**, soaring over huge distances in its search for food.

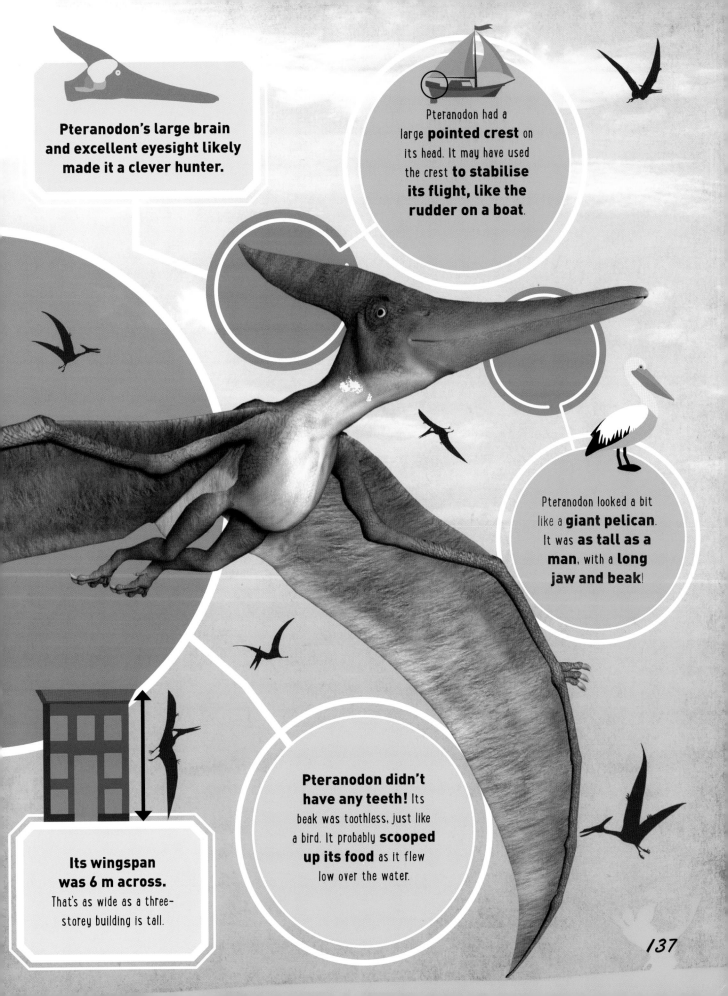

Pteranodon's large brain and excellent eyesight likely made it a clever hunter.

Pteranodon had a large **pointed crest** on its head. It may have used the crest **to stabilise its flight, like the rudder on a boat**.

Pteranodon looked a bit like a **giant pelican**. It was **as tall as a man**, with a **long jaw and beak**!

Pteranodon didn't have any teeth! Its beak was toothless, just like a bird. It probably **scooped up its food** as it flew low over the water.

Its wingspan was 6 m across. That's as wide as a three-storey building is tall.

HUGE HATZEGOPTERYX

Hatzegopteryx is one of the **largest flying animals** to have ever lived. Its home was Hateg Island, near modern-day Romania. This pterosaur was **over 5 m tall** and hunted both in the air and on land.

Hatzegopteryx, pronounced HAT-zeh-GOP-teh-rix, means Hateg basin wing.

Hatzegopteryx's skull alone was **3 m long**! That is about **one-and-a-half times the length of a bed**.

Hatzegopteryx had **hollow bones** that helped it **fly** and made it very **light**. It probably only **weighed about 250 kg**. That's about the same as a **calf**.

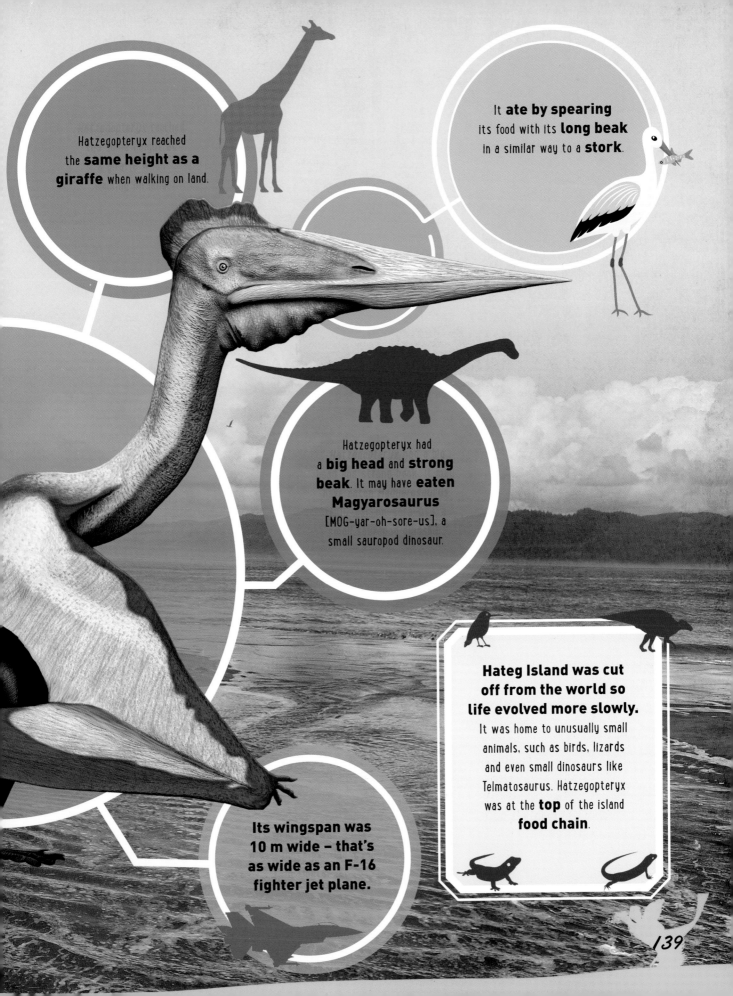

Hatzegopteryx reached the **same height as a giraffe** when walking on land.

It **ate by spearing** its food with its **long beak** in a similar way to a **stork**.

Hatzegopteryx had a **big head** and **strong beak**. It may have **eaten Magyarosaurus** [MOG-yar-oh-sore-us], a small sauropod dinosaur.

Its wingspan was **10 m wide – that's as wide as an F-16 fighter jet plane.**

Hateg Island was cut off from the world so life evolved more slowly. It was home to unusually small animals, such as birds, lizards and even small dinosaurs like Telmatosaurus. Hatzegopteryx was at the **top** of the island **food chain**.

ENORMOUS WINGED QUETZALCOATLUS

One of the most famous pterosaurs is also one of the **biggest flying animals** to have ever lived on Earth. Quetzalcoatlus cast an enormous shadow as it flew through the skies during the **Cretaceous period**.

While Quetzalcoatlus was one of the biggest pterosaurs, it didn't weigh a lot for its size – only **about 250 kg**. Its **bones** were hollow and thin – **as thin as a playing card**. This helped it take to the skies.

Pronounced KET-sal-co-atil-us, **Quetzalcoatlus** is named after the **Aztec feathered serpent god**, Quetzalcoatl, from the area of modern day Mexico.

Quetzalcoatlus could snap up small or baby dinosaurs in its huge jaws.

Quetzalcoatlus had a **very long neck** – about **3 m long**. That's **as long as a camel.**

At 2.5 m long, its head was the size of a small car!

Quetzalcoatlus may have used its **long, toothless jaw** to **dig for food** in the sand.

This pterosaur had a **bony crest made of keratin.**

Quetzalcoatlus possibly glided rather than flew.

Some scientists suggest it could fly at speeds of **up to 130 kph. That's as fast as a golden eagle.**

This pterosaur's **enormous wingspan** was over **10 m wide.** The bird with the biggest wingspan today is the **wandering albatross.** Its **wingspan** is only **3 m across.**

PRETTY PTERODAUSTRO

Pterodaustro was a flying reptile that lived near lakes in what is now **Argentina in South America**. It **hunted** for small crustaceans, such as **shrimp**, as it waded through the shallow waters.

Pterodaustro, pronounced TEH-roe-daws-trow, means southern wing.

A fossilised Pterodaustro **egg** has been **found with the baby** Pterodaustro still **inside**!

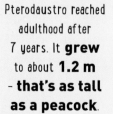

Pterodaustro reached adulthood after 7 years. It **grew** to about **1.2 m** - **that's as tall as a peacock**.

Its **long head and neck** but **short feet** meant it would have needed a long run-up to fly, **like a swan** taking off from water today.

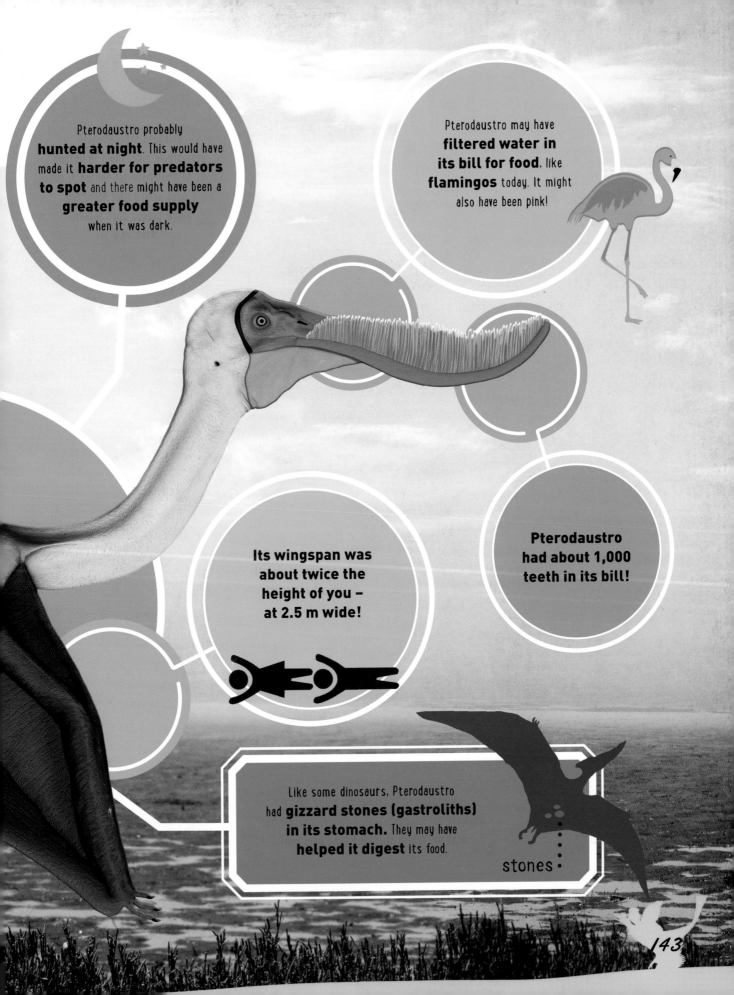

Pterodaustro probably **hunted at night**. This would have made it **harder for predators to spot** and there might have been a **greater food supply** when it was dark.

Pterodaustro may have **filtered water in its bill for food**, like **flamingos** today. It might also have been pink!

Its wingspan was about twice the height of you – at 2.5 m wide!

Pterodaustro had about 1,000 teeth in its bill!

Like some dinosaurs, Pterodaustro had **gizzard stones (gastroliths) in its stomach.** They may have **helped it digest** its food.

stones

QUICK FANCY FACTS

What made many pterosaurs stand out from the crowd? It was their bold and elaborate head crests. Here are some more fancy flying reptiles!

CAIUAJARA

PRONUNCIATION: kai-wua-JAR-a
LENGTH: Unknown
WINGSPAN: 2.3 m
LIVED: Late Cretaceous
LOCATION: Brazil
DIET: Fruit
FACT: Caiuajara had a crest shaped like the sail of a yacht.

TUPANDACTYLUS

PRONUNCIATION: too-PAN-dak-till-us
LENGTH: Unknown
WINGSPAN: 5 m
LIVED: Cretaceous period
LOCATION: Brazil
DIET: Fish
FACT: Tupandactylus' huge sail-like crest could reach up to a metre in height.

NEMICOLOPTERUS

PRONUNCIATION: neh-mi-COL-opteh-rus
LENGTH: about 10 cm
WINGSPAN: 25 cm
LIVED: Cretaceous period
LOCATION: China
DIET: Insects
FACT: Nemicolopterus was the smallest known pterosaur. It was no bigger than a sparrow.

TAPEJARA

PRONUNCIATION: tap-eh-JAR-a
LENGTH: Unknown
WINGSPAN: 3.5 m
LIVED: Cretaceous period
LOCATION: Brazil
DIET: Fish
FACT: Tapejara had an elaborate head crest that was up to a metre tall. It may have used it for mating displays, just like a male peacock uses his tail feathers.

NYCTOSAURUS

PRONUNCIATION: nic-toe-SORE-us
LENGTH: 37 cm
WINGSPAN: At least 2 m
LIVED: Cretaceous period
LOCATION: USA
DIET: Fish
FACT: Nyctosaurus had two long bones sticking out of its head, like deer antlers.

THALASSODROMEUS

PRONUNCIATION: tha-lass-a-DRO-me-us
LENGTH: 1.8 m
WINGSPAN: 4.5-5 m
LIVED: Cretaceous period
LOCATION: Brazil
DIET: Fish and meat
FACT: Thalassodromeus had a crest three times larger than its skull! It is one of the largest pterosaur crests.

DINOSAUR
BONES AND FOSSILS

THE WORLD OF THE DINOSAURS

Dinosaurs successfully ruled Earth for more than 150 million years. Palaeontologists learn about these prehistoric creatures from the **remains** they left behind. These remains are called **fossils**.

The first dinosaur to be described scientifically was **Megalosaurus** [MEG-ah-low-sore-us] in 1824.

New fossils are being found all the time. Palaeontologists are uncovering about **50 new species** of dinosaur a year. That's an average of nearly one a week!

Scientists have ways of **identifying** dinosaur bones. For example, they might recognise the **shape** of the bone or tooth from a previous fossil find.

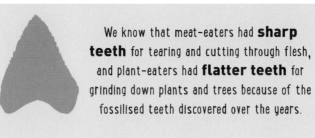

We know that meat-eaters had **sharp teeth** for tearing and cutting through flesh, and plant-eaters had **flatter teeth** for grinding down plants and trees because of the fossilised teeth discovered over the years.

New **technology** means scientists can learn more and more about dinosaurs from their fossil remains. For example, **CT scans,** which use X-rays to **reconstruct** living or fossilised things in three dimensions using computers, are being used to **look inside** dinosaur skulls.

A recent CT scan of a **Tyrannosaurus rex** revealed it had large internal sense organs. This mighty meat-eater had a great sense of smell!

BONE FOSSILS

Fossils finds can be split into **bone fossils** and **trace fossils**. Bone fossils tell us about an animal's body. They are the most common kind of fossil and include body parts such as teeth, bones, claws and, more rarely, soft body tissue.

Most dead animals do not become fossils. Usually, when an animal dies, its body **decays** and **breaks down,** but occasionally the right conditions mean the process of **fossilisation** can begin.

1. A dead animal's flesh is eaten or rots away.

2. Its skeleton sinks into mud or sand.

Bone fossils can be split into four categories:

Articulated skeleton: An almost complete skeleton with its bones still joined together.

Associated skeleton: When bones are found to be from the same animal but have been broken apart.

Isolated bone: One bone. such as a thigh bone (femur).

Float: A piece of bone.

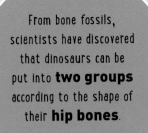

From bone fossils, scientists have discovered that dinosaurs can be put into **two groups** according to the shape of their **hip bones**.

Saurischians [SAW-ris-kee-uns] were lizard-hipped dinosaurs. Most lizard-hipped dinosaurs, such as **T. rex** and **Velociraptor** had hip bones (in orange) that pointed forwards and down. All meat-eaters (and some plant-eaters) were **lizard-hipped dinosaurs**.

Ornithischians [awr-nuh-THIS-kee-uns] are often called **bird-hipped dinosaurs**. Bird-hipped dinosaurs were all **plant-eaters**, such as **Stegosaurus** and **Triceratops**. They had hip bones (in orange) that pointed backwards.

3. Layers of mud and sand bury the skeleton.

4. Over millions of years, the sediment hardens to become rock and the animal is preserved as a fossil.

5. Scientists discover the fossil.

TRACE FOSSILS

Occasionally the fossils of **footprints** or **dinosaur poo** are found. These are known as 'trace fossils' because they help us learn about a dinosaur's **behaviour**.

Trace fossils formed when a **footprint** or **dinosaur poo** was left in soft mud or sand and quickly dried before it could be washed away. It was then covered in layers of rock, sand and mud, which **preserved** the fossil.

Fossilised tracks can reveal if a dinosaur walked on two feet or four, how quickly it moved and if it lived alone or in herds.

Fossilised poo, **coprolite**, can help palaeontologists learn what dinosaurs ate. Coprolites are very rare because dinosaur poo would have usually been washed away quickly.

One of the **largest** dinosaur **coprolites** ever found was 44 cm long and 13 cm wide! That's about the same length as two footballs side by side. This enormous poo contained **bone** that the dinosaur had eaten, so scientists think this coprolite came from a large meat-eating dinosaur, such as **T. rex**.

Coprolites from dinosaurs from the Cretaceous period (146 to 65 mya) such as Maiasaura have been found with **small burrows** in them. Creatures that fed on the poo, such as **dung beetles**, probably made the holes.

In 2018, researchers from the University of Edinburgh found dozens of **footprints** on the Isle of Skye in Scotland. Some of these footprints belonged to huge **sauropods**. Each track was up to 70 cm wide – that's as big as a **car tyre**!

Theropods left tracks at the site, too. The footprints crossed up and down across ground that would have once been **water**, suggesting these dinosaurs often moved in and out of the shallows.

In 2005, the world's **smallest dinosaur footprint**, just 1.8 cm long, was found on the Isle of Skye. Scientists aren't sure which dinosaur it belonged to.

North America has been a hot spot for fossil hunters. More than **400 fossils** have been found in Alberta, **Canada** alone, including **Albertosaurus**, **Ankylosaurus** and **Troodon**.

One dinosaur bone bed in Utah, **USA**, is home to over **10,000 bones**. Some of these bones are believed to be from plant-eaters who became **trapped in the mud** at the edge of a lake. They attracted the attention of predators who also became trapped.

North America

DINOSAURS AROUND THE WORLD

We know that, over the **Mesozoic era**, the supercontinent **Pangaea** began to break apart. As it **split**, dinosaurs moved across the land. Pangaea became Earth's seven **continents** and dinosaur **fossils** have been found on every one.

South America

There have been some important recent dinosaur discoveries in **South America**. Small pieces of bone found in **Argentina** belong to **Giganotosaurus**. This helped scientists understand it was bigger and fiercer than T. rex and that it lived millions of years earlier. It also possibly hunted the enormous **Argentinosaurus,** which lived there at the same time.

Europe is where the fossil remains of large dinosaur teeth were found by Mary and Gideon Mantell in England in 1822. They were the **first fossils** ever found of the dinosaur **Iguanodon**.

Lots of dinosaur discoveries of the 20th and 21st centuries have been unearthed in **Asia**. **Jianianhualong** [Jee-an-yan-hoo-ah-long] is a slender **raptor** dinosaur that was covered in **feathers** and even had wings. It was first found in 2017 and scientists think it looked a bit like a chicken!

Europe

Asia

Africa

A fossil of the mighty **Spinosaurus** was first found in the Sahara Desert in **Egypt** in 1912.

In **Lesotho** in 1978, the first fossil of small and speedy **Lesothosaurus** [le-SO-toe-sore-us] was uncovered.

Oceania

Dinosaurs that lived in **Antarctica** would have enjoyed a warmer climate than the icy weather the area is known for today. The continent would have been covered in trees, rather than ice, and home to dinosaurs such as **Cryolophosaurus** [cry-o-LOAF-oh-sore-us] and the enormous Jurassic sauropod **Glacialisaurus** [GLAY-see-al-ee-SORE-us].

Dinosaur Cove in Victoria, **Australia** is another important dinosaur site. William Hamilton Ferguson discovered the first dinosaur fossil in Australia at the site in 1903. An almost complete skeleton of the dinosaur **Minmi** [min-me] was found there in 1989.

Antarctica

155

IGUANODON BONES

Iguanodon fossils have been found in many parts of the world. These dinosaurs left behind **bone fossils** and **trace fossils** that tell us a great deal about the bodies and behaviours of these **large plant-eaters.**

First discovered: England, 1822

Discovered by:
Mary and Gideon Mantell

First fossil: Teeth

Fossils found around the world:
Belgium, England, USA

The first bones found were fossilised **teeth**. They looked similar to **iguana** teeth, but **ten times bigger**! Gideon Mantell thought the bones belonged to a giant prehistoric lizard, so he named this new creature Iguanodon. Experts disagreed and said the teeth belonged to a mammal, perhaps a rhinoceros!

Over the next 20 years, Gideon found **more teeth and bones.** Eventually he was able to **persuade** the experts that he was right — the bones did belong to a **giant prehistoric lizard** — a dinosaur!

Early drawings of Iguanodon show the dinosaur's **tail dragging** along the ground, like an **iguana's tail**. Now, experts think Iguanodon's heavy tail was **held stiffly** off the ground while the dinosaur walked on two or four legs.

Iguana

Iguanodon's **skull** was thin, tall and narrow. Its **eyes** were high on its head to help it see far and wide.

Iguanodon had a very long **tongue** and a flexible top **jaw**. As the lower jaw pressed into the top jaw, the top jaw could bend outwards to crush up food between its **teeth**.

Iguanodon had **four-fingered hands**. The three middle fingers were joined together by a piece of flesh but the fourth could move easily. The dinosaur's long, spiky **thumb claw** is now its most famous feature.

Iguanodon had no **front teeth**, only a **beak** made from **keratin.** Its strong 5-cm-long back teeth could break down plant material easily.

Fossilised **track marks** found in England show Iguanodon walking on **two legs** (bipedal) but it's believed it could walk on **four legs** (quadrupedal) too. The dinosaur's ability to walk on two or four legs would have come in handy. Iguanodon may have found and eaten its food as it walked slowly on four legs but if it needed to **escape** a predator, it could get away quickly on its two longer back legs.

ANKYLOSAURUS BONES

Ankylosaurus was the **largest** of the armoured dinosaurs, called **Ankylosaurids.** No complete skeleton of this mighty dinosaur has been found – **yet.**

First discovered: Montana, USA, 1906

Discovered by: Barnum Brown

First fossils: Rib, bits of armour, part of a shoulder, sections of vertebrae and the top of a skull

Fossils found around the world:
Canada, USA

Ankylosaurus is famous for its **bony plates** and **scutes** and its deadly **tail club**. The fossilised remains of two tail clubs have been found. Both are damaged, as though they had hit something hard, possibly when used for **defence**.

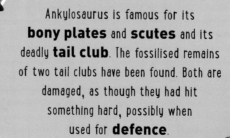

Most Ankylosaurus **fossils** were fossilised **upside-down**. Dinosaur experts were keen to find out why. The most likely answer is the **bloat and float theory**. The dinosaurs' bodies washed into rivers and seas, where they became bloated and eventually floated, before sinking to the bottom of the water.

The two Ankylosaurus **skulls** found so far each had large internal **sense organs**, so Ankylosaurus probably had a strong sense of **smell** to help it find food.

Ankylosaurus **skulls** were triangular with a narrow **beak** at the end and no sign of any grinding teeth. This meant Ankylosaurus could strip **leaves** from plants but it could not grind down large plant material.

The partial **skeletons** reveal a large space where Ankylosaurus's **stomach** and **intestines** would have been. The space was probably very big to allow the dinosaur to **digest** the huge amount of **plant** material – about 60 kg – it needed to eat every day to support its size.

Ankylosaurus was one of the **last dinosaurs**, living at the end of the Cretaceous period. Some experts have suggested its **armour** could be an **evolutionary** change that was slowly happening in plant-eating dinosaurs in order to **survive** in a world ruled by mighty meat-eaters, such as T. rex.

STEGOSAURUS BONES

Stegosaurus could reach up to 9 m long – almost the size of a bus. It is famous for the **bony plates** that ran down its back and tail, making it seem even bigger than it was!

First discovered: USA, 1876

Discovered by: M.P. Felch and named by Othniel Charles Marsh in 1877

First fossil: Bone fragments

Fossils found around the world: USA

Stegosaurus had a bendy **tail** with those long, recognisable **spikes** on the end, **thagomizers**. Fossil finds of some of these spikes show **damage**, supporting the idea that the dinosaur used them as a **weapon** to defend itself.

Scientists have also found thagomizer puncture **wounds** on the fossil remains of Stegosaurus's main **predator** - Allosaurus.

The surfaces of the **plates** on Stegosaurus's back and tail were covered in tiny grooves where **blood vessels** might have been. This could suggest blood passed through the plates as a way of **cooling** the dinosaur down or **warming** it up.

Othniel Charles Marsh, the scientist who gave Stegosaurus its name, originally thought the **fossil bones** belonged to an animal that lived in **water**, like a turtle. He thought the dinosaur's bony plates lay flat on its back, a bit like the tiles on a roof.

Discoveries of more complete skeletons led experts to realise that the bony **plates** stood **upright** in two **rows**, in an alternating pattern.

A space in the **hip** of early Stegosaurus fossils led scientists to think that Stegosaurus had a **brain** in its tail that controlled the lower half of its body. They wondered if it gave the dinosaur a burst of speed when under attack. Other experts quickly dismissed the theory of an extra brain in the dinosaur's bottom!

Stegosaurus had a small **skull** and **brain** for such a big creature. Its head-down posture meant it probably ate **plants** growing low to the ground. Its teeth were the size of a human fingernail but it had the **bite force** of a cow or sheep.

The most complete **skeleton** of Stegosaurus went on display in the Natural History Museum, London, UK, in 2014. Nicknamed '**Sophie**', the exhibit is **85 per cent complete**, although her head is not real. The real skull is too delicate to display – it is made up of 50 tiny bones. The skeleton was found in 2003 in Wyoming, USA.

TRICERATOPS BONES

Triceratops, with its three enormous **horns** and large **frill** around its head, is perhaps one of the most well known dinosaurs. Several fascinating Triceratops fossil **excavations** have taken place across North America.

First discovered:
USA, 1887

Discovered by: Unknown

First fossil: Partial horn

Fossils found around the world: North America

When the **first fossil** was found, it was thought that the bone came from a giant prehistoric **bison** and the animal was named *bison alticornis*. It was renamed Triceratops in 1889 after the palaeontologist John Bell Hatcher found the first Triceratops skull in 1888.

So far, more than **50 skulls** and some **partial skeletons** of Triceratops have been found, including the **skulls** of young Triceratops.

T. rex **bite marks** on Triceratops fossil bones show that this meat-eater managed to **feast** on Triceratops from time to time. That would have been quite a meal!

In 1997, a fossil was discovered with a **horn bitten off** and bite marks that belonged to a **T. rex**. The wounds had healed, which means that this Triceratops had successfully **fought off** an attack from a large meat-eating predator.

In 2017, builders found fossil bones of a Triceratops when working on a new fire and police station in Colorado, USA. Further digging revealed the main parts of the **skull**, both **horns** above the eyes and parts of its lower **jaw**. **Vertebrae**, ribs and a shoulder blade were also excavated from the same site.

The 2017 discovery was exciting because the **skull** of Triceratops is often found on its own. It is rare to find the skull alongside other bones. This is probably because once the dinosaur has died, the smaller parts of the body **decay** or get **eaten** by **scavengers**, but the strong skull bones stay around for a while.

There is **debate** amongst scientists as to whether **Triceratops** and another dinosaur **Torosaurus** [tor-oh-SORE-us] are in fact the same dinosaur. One expert has suggested that Torosaurus, whose **head frill** has large **holes** in it, is simply Triceratops in old age, but other scientists disagree.

DIPLODOCUS BONES

There have been **lots of fossils** of Diplodocus found over the years, including some **near-complete skeletons.** Most have been discovered in the Rocky Mountain area of Colorado, Montana, Utah and Wyoming in the USA.

First discovered: Colorado, USA, 1877

Discovered by: Benjamin Mudge and Samuel W. Williston

First fossil: Vertebrae and other bones

Fossils found around the world: USA

In the early 20th century, experts believed Diplodocus walked with **sprawled legs** like a crocodile or lizard. This theory was quickly disproven in the 1920s.

In the 1930s, fossil **footprints** suggested the dinosaur had four thick, strong **legs** that went **straight** down under its body and allowed it to move slowly, a bit like an **elephant**.

In 1905, a cast of a Diplodocus **skeleton** was given to the Natural History Museum in London. It was nicknamed 'Dippy'. It was originally displayed with its **tail** down but, in 1995, after **new research** showed that the tail would have been lifted up to balance the neck, Dippy's tail was raised up high. Dippy sometimes goes on tour around the UK.

In October 2018, scientists revealed that a **skull** found in 2010 in Montana, USA, belonged to a **juvenile** Diplodocus. Less than 12 Diplodocus skulls have been dug up to date so this tiny one, nicknamed 'Andrew', is a very **rare** discovery. It is just **25.5 cm** wide and experts think the dinosaur was less than **five years old** when it died.

Dippy is **cleaned** every two years. It takes two people two days to clean Dippy's **292 bones**.

Andrew's **skull** was found in a **bone bed** with at least 16 other similar juvenile dinosaurs. The bones are dotted with **mud**, which might suggest the dinosaur herd **died** in a **flood**.

Diplodocus's neck alone had **15 vertebrae** and it had a row of extra **bones** underneath its **spine**, which probably helped **support** the dinosaur's long **neck** and spine.

The **longest near-complete** dinosaur **skeleton** we have is of a Diplodocus. Other dinosaurs were bigger but we have not yet found a complete set of bones from these species.

VELOCIRAPTOR BONES

This fierce, turkey-sized dinosaur was covered in **feathers** and had fearsome **claws** on its back feet, used to stab its prey and prevent it from escaping.

Henry Fairfield Osborn was an American scientist who first described Velociraptor in 1924. He assumed the **fossilised claw** was from the dinosaur's **hand**. We now know it was the **second toe** of the dinosaur's foot.

First discovered: Gobi Desert, Mongolia, 1924

Discovered by: Henry Fairfield Osborn

First fossils: Claw and a crushed skull

Fossils found around the world: Mongolia and China

Velociraptor's **tail bones** were **fused together** so the tail was long and stiff to **help** it run, hunt and jump on its prey.

Velociraptor had **long legs** for its size. They were strong and muscly so could have moved at speeds of up to **65 kph** - quicker than the world's fastest man, Usain Bolt! His top speed ever recorded is 45 kph.

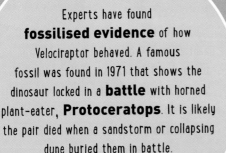

Experts have found **fossilised evidence** of how Velociraptor behaved. A famous fossil was found in 1971 that shows the dinosaur locked in a **battle** with horned plant-eater, **Protoceratops**. It is likely the pair died when a sandstorm or collapsing dune buried them in battle.

Another **rare** Velociraptor **fossil** was found in 2012. Inside the skeleton of the young Velociraptor was the **remains** of its last **meal** - the broken bone of a **pterosaur**. The **flying reptile** would have been too big and dangerous to hunt, so the dinosaur probably **scavenged** the bone from the creature after it had died.

Quill knobs are tiny bumps on the wing bones of some modern-day birds. They help hold flight **feathers** in place. The discovery of quill knobs on a Velociraptor fossil found in 2017 indicate this dinosaur had long feathers that stretched over its arms.

Further evidence that Velociraptor had **feathers** can be found with its close relatives **Microraptor** and **Zhenyuanlong**. Fossils of both of these dinosaurs have been found with feathers intact.

Despite its wing-like **feathered arms**, Velociraptor couldn't fly. It probably had feathers to keep it **warm**, for use during **mating displays** or to keep its **eggs warm**.

TYRANNOSAURUS REX BONES

Tyrannosaurus rex is considered the ultimate **carnivore**. This famously fierce **predator** left evidence of its **hunting skills** inside the bones and bodies of some of its victims.

First discovered: Hill Creek Formation, Montana, USA, 1902

Discovered by: Barnum Brown

First fossil: Fragments of bone

Fossils found around the world: North America

Barnum Brown discovered the first recognised fossils of T. rex in Montana, USA. Only **seven T. rex fossils** that are more than **half-complete** have been found since, but we still **know a lot** about this dinosaur.

Experts know T. rex was a fierce meat-eater because its **bite marks** have been found on the fossil bones of **Triceratops** and **Edmontosaurus**.

Coprolites from T. rex revealed these dinosaurs weren't too fussy – they didn't just eat flesh but **crunched through bone** too.

In 2013, a study described the finding of a **T. rex tooth** in the **tailbone** of a duckbilled dinosaur. The bone had **healed** over the tooth, suggesting the **prey** had got away, taking a bit of its predator with it!

T. rex is known for its **short arms** and scientists still **debate** what the dinosaur used these for. Could they **grasp** struggling **prey** or help the dinosaur get up and down from the ground? Perhaps they had **no function**, like the wings of **flightless birds** today, such as an ostrich.

Studies of fossils show that T. rex's **bite force** meant it could easily bite through **bone**. In 1996, scientists described one fossil of a **Triceratops** pelvis that was covered in more than **50 T. rex bite marks**!

Some scientists have suggested a T. rex's **arms** were more **useful** when it was a **juvenile**. Its short arms would have been more in **proportion** with the rest of its **body** and may have been helpful when **hunting** or **scavenging** prey. As the dinosaur grew, it didn't need to use its arms to hunt or find food.

In 2014, scientists may have found the **trackways** of three tyrannosaurs in Canada. They appear to have been moving in the **same direction** at the **same time**. These individuals may have been **living** as a group or even **hunting** as a **pack**. One animal was missing a **claw** from its left foot, which may have been a **battle wound**.

SPINOSAURUS BONES

Spinosaurus was a mighty hunter, too – it was thinner than T. rex, but with **longer forearms** and a huge **sail-like** structure on its back. Its bones tell us it may have been at home in the **water** as well.

First discovered: Egypt 1911–1914

Discovered by: Ernst Stromer

First fossil: Two partial skeletons

Fossils found around the world: Morocco, Egypt

The first, and most complete, Spinosaurus bones were found in the **Sahara Desert** in Egypt. The fossils were **displayed** in a museum in **Munich** in Germany but the building was **bombed** during the **Second World War** (1939-45) and the fossils were **destroyed**. All that was left were a few drawings, Stromer's field notes and some photographs.

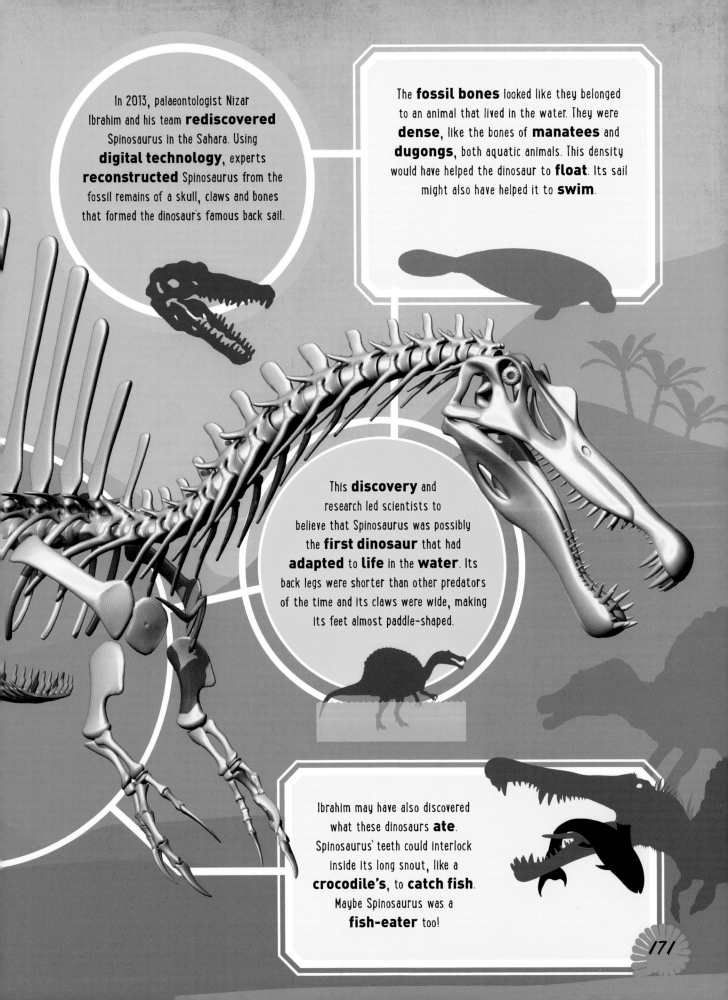

In 2013, palaeontologist Nizar Ibrahim and his team **rediscovered** Spinosaurus in the Sahara. Using **digital technology**, experts **reconstructed** Spinosaurus from the fossil remains of a skull, claws and bones that formed the dinosaur's famous back sail.

The **fossil bones** looked like they belonged to an animal that lived in the water. They were **dense**, like the bones of **manatees** and **dugongs**, both aquatic animals. This density would have helped the dinosaur to **float**. Its sail might also have helped it to **swim**.

This **discovery** and research led scientists to believe that Spinosaurus was possibly the **first dinosaur** that had **adapted** to **life** in the **water**. Its back legs were shorter than other predators of the time and its claws were wide, making its feet almost paddle-shaped.

Ibrahim may have also discovered what these dinosaurs **ate**. Spinosaurus' teeth could interlock inside its long snout, like a **crocodile's**, to **catch fish**. Maybe Spinosaurus was a **fish-eater** too!

DINOSAUR DETECTIVES

Palaeontologists are scientists who study fossils. There have been many famous dinosaur fossil hunters over the years. Here are some of them!

OTHNIEL CHARLES MARSH (1831–1899) AND EDWARD DRINKER COPE (1840–1897)

During the Great Dinosaur Rush in USA, these two men discovered over 150 species in their fight to be the best dinosaur hunter. This battle, called the Bone Wars, lasted until Cope's death in 1897. But the pair did make a few mistakes along the way. Marsh publicly humiliated Cope by revealing he had placed the head of Elasmosaurus on its tail! The famous battle lost both men their fortunes but science learned much from their numerous discoveries.

MARY ANNING (1799–1847)

Mary and her family hunted for fossils on the beaches of England and sold them to wealthy tourists. She discovered many famous dinosaurs and prehistoric creatures, including Iguanodon and ichthyosaurs, but because she was poor and a woman, nobody paid much attention to her work. Today, we recognise Anning as an important palaeontologist in her own right.

BARNUM BROWN (1873-1963)

Barnum Brown spent most of his adult life hunting for fossils around the world. He was the first scientist to find a partial skeleton of Tyrannosaurus rex and would later find a more complete specimen that would form the basis for our understanding of this famous dinosaur.

DONG ZHIMING

Dong Zhiming is a leading palaeontologist in China and around the world. He made his first dinosaur fossil find at 26. It was a vertebra from a sauropod, the most gigantic of dinosaurs to have walked the Earth. He has since uncovered many dinosaurs in China and named about 20 dinosaurs himself.

PATRICIA VICKERS-RICH

Patricia and her husband Tim Rich have uncovered many dinosaurs in Australia's Dinosaur Cove - such as Leaellynasaura and Timimus. both named after their children. Her work has helped prove that some dinosaurs could survive in the very cold conditions of Cretaceous Australia - a very different climate to today!

DR KAREN CHIN

Dr Chin is an American palaeontologist who is one of the world's leading experts on coprolites. Studying coprolites enables her to look for evidence of feeding habits and behaviour and to discover the diets of ancient creatures, including the dinosaurs.

GLOSSARY

adapt(ed) – to adjust or change to suit a new purpose or environment

agile – to move quickly and easily

ammonite – an extinct sea creature, often found as a fossil

ancestor – an early type of animal or plant from which others have evolved

aquatic – relating to water: An aquatic animal is one that lives in water

armour – tough layer that some plants and animals have for protection

Aztecs – a group of people who lived in the area of modern Mexico before the 16th century

bacteria – tiny living things. Some kinds of bacteria live in the digestive system and help break down food

bone bed – an area of rock that contains bones of fossilised animals

brood – to sit on eggs to hatch them

carbon dioxide – a gas, found in the air, without colour or odour that is made up of carbon and oxygen

carcass – the dead body of an animal

carnivore – an animal that eats other animals

climate change – the changing average conditions on Earth, including temperature, winds, and other factors: scientists are concerned that Earth is warming very fast due to human activity

clutch – a group of eggs laid at once

colony – a group of animals or plants living close together

conifer – a kind of tree that produces cones and has needle-like or scale-like leaves

continent – one of the seven major areas of land on Earth

coprolite – fossilised poo

crater – a hole on the surface (of Earth or the Moon, for example) made by something enormous hitting it, such as a meteorite

crest – a growth of feathers, flesh or bone on the head of an animal

Cretaceous period – a period in Earth's history, between 144 and 65 mya

crustacean – a group of mostly water creatures with a body made of sections, such as a crab or shrimp

decay – to rot

descendant – a person, animal or plant that has evolved or descended from a particular ancestor

dietary – of or relating to a diet or to the rules of diet

digest(ion) – the process of breaking down food

dinosaur trap – an area with lots of dinosaur fossils

dominate – to be more powerful than others

dorsal – related to the back, as an organ or part of an animal

downy – covered with fine, soft hair or feathers

drought – a long period without water, when animals, plants and people struggle to survive

dune – a mound of sand formed by the wind

embryo – an unborn or unhatched animal

evidence – the available facts or information

evolution(ary) – the process by which animals and plants have developed and adapted during the history of Earth

evolve – to develop, change or improve by steps

excavated – dug up

expand – to make larger

extinct – when a type of animal dies out completely

fend for – look after

fern – a flowerless plant

filter – to pass water through to remove unwanted material

flock – a number of birds together

flood – a large overflow of water that covers land that is normally dry

floodplain – an area of low-lying ground next to a river or stream

food chain – group of living things (animals and plants) where each member of the group is eaten in turn by another

foraging – searching for food

fossil – the remains of an animal or plant preserved for millions of years

fossilisation – the process of preserving an animal or plant that once lived

frill – a fringe of feathers, hair or bone around the head or neck of an animal

gastrolith (gizzard stone) – a small stone swallowed by some animals to aid digestion

growth spurt – to grow quickly over a short period of time

habitat – the place where an animal or a plant lives

hadrosaurs – a group of plant-eating dinosaurs that lived during the Late Cretaceous period: they walked on two legs, had a beak-like snout and often had a bony crest on their heads

hatch – when an egg opens to produce a young animal

hatchling – a young animal that has recently come out from its egg

herbivore – an animal that eats only plants

herd – a group of animals that live together, often for protection and defence

hunt – to pursue and kill other animals for food

ichthyosaur – a marine reptile from the Mesozoic era

iguana – a tropical lizard

incubated – when a bird or dinosaur sits on a clutch of eggs to keep them warm as they develop

infant – a very young animal

Jurassic period – a period of Earth's history, between 206 and 144 mya

juvenile – a young or baby animal

keratin – a material that makes up hair, feathers, nails, claws etc.

landslide – a collapse of earth and rock

Loch Ness Monster – an aquatic animal that is said to live in the deep waters of Loch Ness in Scotland

Mesozoic Era – a period in Earth's history from 251 to 65 mya, divided into the Triassic, Jurassic and Cretaceous periods, when the dinosaurs lived

meteorite – a piece of rock that falls from space

migrate – to travel from one area to another in search of food or due to the seasons

mollusc – an animal that has a soft body and is often covered with a shell, such as a snail

nocturnal – to be active at night and sleep during the day

pack – a group of wild animals

palaeontologist – a scientist who studies fossils

Pangaea – single, large continent on the Earth, which included all the present seven continents joined together, before they broke up and drifted apart

plates – thin, flat areas that form a structure

plesiosaur – a large marine reptile from the Mesozoic era

pliosaur a plesiosaur with a short neck, large head, and large toothed jaws

predator – an animal that eats other animals

preserve – to keep something as it is

prey – an animal that is eaten by another animal

propel – to push forward

pterosaur – a flying reptile from the Mesozoic era

pup – the young of certain species, including ichthyosaur

quarry – a hole in the ground from which something can be removed

reconstruct – rebuild or make again after something has been damaged or destroyed

reptile – a cold-blooded animal that breathes air and is often covered with scales

retreat – to move back

robust – sturdy and strong

rudder – a piece of wood at the back of the boat that moves from side to side for steering

sandstorm – a strong wind that carries clouds of sand with it, often in a desert

sauropods – a group of dinosaurs that walked on four legs, had long tails and necks, small heads and thick, column-shaped limbs

scavenger – an animal that feeds on dead plants or animals

scute – a thick bony plate on the back of an animal

sediment – soft matter that settles on the surface of the land or on the seabed, and over time may form into rock

snowstorm – a heavy fall of snow with a strong wind

species – a group of animals that are closely related to one another and are very similar

stalk – to pursue another animal, usually while hunting

state fossil – the fossil of one species chosen by an American state

storey – the part of a building where all rooms are on the same level

talon – a claw

thagomizer – an arrangement of spikes on the tails of some dinosaurs

theropod – a group of meat-eating dinosaurs

trackway – a beaten or trodden path. A fossilised trackway is one that has been preserved for millions of years.

Triassic period – a period in Earth's history, between 248 and 206 mya

tsunami – a large ocean wave caused by an underwater volcanic eruption or earthquake

vertebrae – the bones that make up the spine of an animal

volcanic eruption – the sudden expulsion of steam and volcanic material

wingspan – the maximum width of the wings of a flying animal or aircraft

X-ray – a photographic image of the inside of something, especially a body

INDEX

Aegyptosaurus 13
Alamosaurus 44–45
Albertonykus 65
Albertosaurus 71, 154
Allosaurus 16, 17, 26, 31, 43, 51, 52, 64, 65, 69, 88, 160
Amargasaurus 48–49
Ampelosaurus 41
Ankylosaurus 27, 42, 56–57, 154, 158–159
Apatosaurus 16–17, 40, 43, 116
Aquilops 38
Archelon 132
archosaurs 12, 14,
Argentinosaurus 18, 41, 46–47, 154
armour 19, 42, 56–57, 133, 158–159
Austriadactylus 134–135
Barosaurus 27
Baryonyx 85
Beipiaosaurus 83
birds 20, 32, 53, 89, 92–94, 108, 112, 117, 121, 137, 139, 141, 145, 151, 167, 169
Brachiosaurus 16, 39, 41
brains 21, 26, 29, 33, 41, 53, 65, 81, 137, 161
Caiuajara 144
Camarasaurus 40–41
Camptosaurus 39
Canada 30, 60, 86, 102, 154, 158, 169
Centrosaurus 43
Ceratosaurus 30, 51
Cetiosauriscus 41
claws 13, 15, 25, 26, 32, 43, 48, 58–59, 64, 70, 76, 79, 81, 85, 87, 108, 150, 157, 166, 169, 171
Coelophysis 8, 76–77, 88
Compsognathus 33
conifers 17, 36, 49
coprolite(s) 11, 22, 86, 152–153, 169, 173
Corythosaurus 25
Crassigyrinus 132
Cretaceous period 9, 11, 18–19, 23, 25, 28, 33, 39, 46, 58, 72, 78, 80, 85, 100, 102, 108, 112, 128, 136, 140, 144–145, 153, 159
crocodiles 12, 32, 67, 75, 84–85, 100, 102, 121, 164, 171
Cryolophosaurus 155
defences 17, 19, 27, 42–43, 55, 59, 87, 101, 103, 158, 160
Deinonychus 25, 43, 70, 89

Dimorphodon 120–121
Diplodocus 8–9, 20, 30, 50–51, 106–107, 164–165
Dunkleosteus 133
Egg Mountain 103, 110
eggs 8, 22–23, 29, 47, 48, 50, 82, 92–117, 142, 167
Egypt 13, 31, 89, 155, 170
Elasmosaurus 126, 172
embryos 93, 107, 109, 111, 115, 117
Eoraptor 15, 70
Eudimorphodon 135,
Euoplocephalus 19
Eurhinosaurus 125
extinction, dinosaur 93, 129
eyes (eyesight) 26, 43, 65, 66, 70, 73, 77, 101, 113, 114, 123, 125, 137, 157, 163
feathers 13, 21, 65, 66, 72, 75, 78, 82, 82–83, 97, 109, 112–113, 117, 140, 145, 155, 166–167
ferns 36, 49
fish-eaters 84–85, 134, 171
footprints 44, 99, 116, 152–153, 164
fossils 11, 13–15, 20, 22, 23, 25, 27, 30–33, 36, 40, 41, 44, 45, 52, 58, 60–61, 69, 71, 76, 84–89, 95, 99, 100, 109, 110–113, 115, 116–117, 125, 127–129, 131, 133, 142, 148–173
Gallimimus 60, 68
Gargoyleosaurus 38
gastroliths 41, 53, 143
Giganotosaurus 18, 21, 30, 46, 80–81, 154
gizzard stones 143
Glacialisaurus 155
Globidens 128
Gobi Desert 60, 104, 109, 113, 166
hadrosaurs 19, 110
Hainosaurus 128–129
Hateg Island 138–139
Hatzegopteryx 138–139
head crests 19, 25, 60, 135, 137, 141, 144–145
herds 19, 22–25, 44–45, 47, 55, 60, 69, 44, 95, 107, 110, 152, 165
Hesperonychus 64
hip 151, 161
horn 13, 19, 42–43, 54–55, 61, 100–101, 162–163, 167
hunting in packs 25, 70–71, 76, 82, 135, 169

Hypacrosaurus 92–93
ichthyosaurs 9, 114–115, 120, 122–125, 172
Ichthyosaurus 124–125
Iguanodon 11, 13, 31, 58–59, 71, 155–157, 172
Jianianhualong 155
Jurassic period 8–9, 11, 16–17, 19, 33, 39, 50, 88–89
juveniles 23, 45, 94–95, 97, 99, 110, 101, 107, 110, 111, 165, 168,
Kentrosaurus 42
Kronosaurus 127
Leedsichthys 133
Lesothosaurus 61, 155
Liopleurodon 122–123, 133
Loch Ness Monster 123
Magyarosaurus 139
Maiasaura 23, 110–111, 117, 153
Mamenchisaurus 21, 41
mammals 8, 17, 29, 33, 68, 131, 156
Medusaceratops Lokii 13
Megalodon 130–131
Megalosaurus 148
Megaraptor 71
Mesozoic era 8–9, 36, 114, 116, 120, 126, 134, 154
Micropachycephalosaurus 38
Microraptor 64–65, 89, 20–21, 167
Minmi 61, 155
mosasaurs 127–129, 132
museums 32, 161, 165, 170
Mussaurus 15, 116
Nemicolopterus 145
nests 22–23, 50, 78, 82, 92–93, 96–113, 116
Nigersaurus 39, 41
Nothronychus 117
Nyasasaurus parringtoni 8
Nyctosaurus 145
Odobenocetops 131
ornithischians 151
Orodromeus 23, 103
Oviraptor 23, 108–109, 112–113
Oviraptorosauria 117
Owen, Richard 12
palaeontologist(s) 54, 67, 85, 86, 148, 152, 162, 171–173
Pangaea 9–11, 16, 154
Parasaurolophus 19, 30, 60
parenting 23, 94–95, 105, 108–116
Pentaceratops 21
phytosaurs 14

plants 10–11, 16–17, 18, 20, 23, 24–25, 27, 28–29, 30, 33, 36–41, 44, 49, 51, 52–61, 68–69, 73, 98, 100, 103, 106, 110–111, 149, 151, 154, 156–157, 159, 161, 167
Plateosaurus 8, 15, 31
plates 19, 27, 33, 52–53, 56, 126, 133, 158, 160–161
plesiosaurs 120–121, 123, 126–127, 129
pliosaurs 121, 122, 126–127
Postosuchus 12
Pouech, Jean-Jacques 93, 117
Protoceratops 87, 93, 104–105, 109, 167
Psittacosaurus 116
Pteranodon 136–137
Pterodaustro 142–143
pterosaurs 9, 18, 87, 120–121, 134–135, 136, 138, 140–141, 144–145, 167
Pterygotus 133
Puertasaurus 24–25
Quetzalcoatlus 140–141
Rapetosaurus 94–95
Repenomamus robustus 116
Rhoetosaurus 41
Saltopus 15
Sanajeh indicus 107
saurischians 151
Saurophaganax 67
sauropods 13, 16–17, 20–21, 24, 27, 40–41, 44–47, 106–107, 139, 153, 155, 173
Sauroposeidon 21, 33
scavengers 25, 26, 66, 68–69, 73, 163, 167, 169
Scelidosaurus 27
Sciurumimus 117
sharks 32, 67, 74, 115, 129, 130–133
Shastasaurus 123
Sinornithomimus dongi 95
skin 13, 26–27, 42, 52, 66, 81, 134
skulls 23, 42, 49, 54, 61, 75, 77, 97, 101, 113, 138, 145, 149, 156–167, 171
snakes 13, 106–107, 124, 129
spikes 10, 13, 19, 27, 42, 52, 56–57, 160
Spinosaurus 13, 31, 69, 74–75, 89, 155, 170–171
Stegoceras 42
Stegosaurus 8, 17, 21, 27, 33, 36, 52–53, 98–99, 151, 160–161
Stethacanthus 133

Stromer, Ernst 170
Stygimoloch 61
Styracosaurus 37
Suchomimus 84–85
tails 13, 17, 20, 25, 27, 40, 42–43, 50–51, 52, 56, 66, 75, 76, 80, 106, 111, 114, 117, 121, 124, 128, 130, 134, 136, 145, 157, 158, 160–161, 165, 166, 169, 172
tail clubs 27, 42, 56, 158
Tapejara 145
technology 149, 171
teeth 15, 26–27, 37, 39, 40–41, 42, 47, 49, 51, 53, 55, 57, 59, 67, 68–69, 76, 79, 81, 84–85, 96–97, 111, 115, 120–123, 125, 127, 129, 131, 132–133, 135, 136–137, 143, 149, 150, 155, 156–157, 159, 161, 171
Temnodontosaurus 123
Tenontosaurus 25, 70
thagomizers 52, 160
Thalassodromeus 145
theropods 13, 21, 64, 71, 96, 153
tracks 45, 153–153, 157, 169
Triceratops 9, 30, 36–37, 54–55, 69, 86, 100–101, 104, 151, 162–163, 168–169
Troodon 23, 33, 65, 102–103, 154
Tupandactylus 144
turtles 92, 95, 106, 126, 129, 131, 132, 161
Tylosaurus 128–129
Tyrannosaurus rex 9, 21, 22, 26, 36–37, 55, 64–65, 67, 68–69, 72–73, 79, 80–81, 86, 95, 96–97, 121, 122, 149, 151, 152, 154, 159, 163, 168–169, 170, 173
UK 58, 161, 165
United States (USA) 30, 60–61, 88–89, 145, 156, 158, 160, 162, 164, 172
Utahraptor 71, 89
Velociraptor 19, 23, 31, 78–79, 87, 112–113, 151, 166–167
vertebrae 47, 51, 52, 158, 163, 164–165, 173
weight 16, 20, 33, 36, 38, 40, 44, 45, 46, 49, 50–51, 57, 59, 60–61, 64, 71, 72–73, 74, 79, 81, 82, 84, 88–89, 93, 97, 98, 100, 111, 126, 130, 138, 140
wings 21, 32, 87, 121, 134–145, 155, 167, 169
Yutyrannus huali 82–83